UNLOCKING
belief

Answering
Questions
Jesus Asks

Katie —
You are, always
have been, a
blessing in my
life. I love you
more than you
will ever know!
Suzanne

Suzanne W. Matthews

Unlocking Belief: Answering Questions Jesus Asks
by Suzanne W. Matthews
© Copyright 2016 Suzanne W. Matthews

Author Blog: *Coffee, Tea and Thee*, www.ctandthee.com

Book Design: *Andrea Wilhelm*

All pivotal questions in the book are in the translation of the *Holman Christian Standard Bible*, from the *HCSB Harmony of the Gospels*. All Bible quotes are from the *Holman Christian Standard Bible* or the *New International Version*, unless otherwise noted.

ISBN: 978-0-692-81878-7

Meet the Author

Erin Cobb Photography

More than twenty-five years ago, Suzanne Matthews found herself at loose ends, searching for God's direction in her life. Her search ended the day she walked in the door of the local Bible Study Fellowship class in Huntsville, Alabama. There she cut her spiritual teeth on expository Bible study and came to love small group study and real life conversations of deep spiritual growth. She went on to teach the BSF Evening Women's Class for fourteen years. After retiring from BSF and from her day job, she wrote *Crossings: Life Lessons from the Book of Joshua*, and has now completed her second Bible study, *Unlocking Belief: Answering Questions Jesus Asks*.

Suzanne is married to the love of her life, Ben, and they have four grown children and seven grandchildren. She loves to read and oil paint, and rarely will turn down a good chocolate dessert. You can keep up with her through her weekly blog at *Coffee, Tea and Thee* (www.ctandthee.com).

Unlocking Belief:
Answering Questions Jesus Asks

is dedicated

to the eleven prayer warriors —
Shay Brannon, Dedra Herod, Judy Howard, Frances Kyser,
Sandy McKenzie, Rica McRoy, May Patterson, Amanda Ragland,
Lee Seeley, Linda Smith, Michelle Vaporis —
who encouraged me to follow the Spirit's lead alone,
and prayed me through delivering eight lectures, writing eight study
guides, and answering *honestly* the eleven questions

to the fifteen women who brought His questions alive —
Celeste Childs, Leslie Cooper, Mary Alice Fann, Amy Harper, Laura Howard,
Janice Johnson, Kim Johnson, Kristi Kelly, Ann Laue, Ingrid Lunsford, Beth McGee,
Ashley Mitchell, Lakshmi Nallamala, Jan Teachey, Charlotte Wessel —
who took the challenge *and* had the courage
to take the veil off their hearts and lives,
and live their faith fully authentically, as iron sharpens iron

and to
The One Who is our Only Answer

Table of Contents

Introduction

People ask me, "Where in the world did you get the idea of answering Jesus' questions?" My answer — "I don't know"; meaning, I cannot explain it. I know that is not what you want to hear, but I have tried to look back and track my thought processes, and I still cannot wrap my head around it or articulate it.

I do remember while studying Focus on the Family's *The Truth Project* that I became incensed at the question Pilate asked Jesus in John 18:38, "What is truth?" Pilate asked it arrogantly, scornfully — he flippantly blew Jesus off, all the while standing in front of The Truth. Somehow that exchange between Pilate and Jesus led me to look at other questions posed to Jesus. I had a moment of stark clarity when I realized Jesus' questions *to others* were far more important than anything asked of Him.

I began to track His questions through the New Testament and plastered hundreds of questions written on pieces of paper on the walls of my studio. I looked at them, and read them over and over. I quickly realized Jesus' communication was built on *asking the question*. I stared at the questions for months, I moved them around on the studio walls, and the questions became chronological. From there, God directed me to eleven pivotal questions; from there, what was on my studio wall became a study. God's stream of thought — who can understand it?

Unlocking Belief is an eight chapter Bible study. We journey through a chronological view of Jesus' life and ministry, stopping to answer eleven questions He asked. Out of the eleven questions, *only three* were ever answered in Scripture.

Each chapter covers a segment of Jesus' life and ends with a pivotal question(s) to answer. *Webster's Dictionary* defines the adjective "pivotal" as "of crucial importance in relation to the development or success of something else." In this study, answering the questions is crucial to spiritual development. *We are the something else.*

Each reflection begins with answering the pivotal question(s) and continues with a short study guide to introduce the next chapter. Each chapter contains at least one key — an aid in unlocking the meaning of the chapter and also a guide to help us unlock the deep recesses of our own belief.

The Key to It All

By far, the most important element of the entire study is *answering* the eleven questions. If you read the chapters or even complete the study guide, but never answer the questions, *Unlocking Belief* is simply a very short, skimming-the-surface, chronological view of Jesus' ministry.

With me (and I have heard the same from others), God's work was done in my heart as I answered each question. One by one. Writing something, coming back to it, chewing on it, starting again, adding to my answers. I believe what helps the most in actually answering the 11 questions is this: **knowing you will never be asked how you answered the question.** Your answers are solely between you and Jesus Christ. There are plenty of ways to have great discussion about Jesus and the questions, yet never be asked to reveal your specific answer. Please do me a favor — if you are ever asked how you answered the questions, say, "The author says that is strictly off limits." And this is why...

One member of the study's focus group said she realized that in other Bible studies she answered her questions knowing that she might be called on to answer. The possibility of being called on influenced her answer. However, knowing that she would *never* be asked how she answered these eleven questions, realizing her answer was completely confidential in Christ, gave her freedom to be totally honest. I found the same to be true. The more questions I answered, the more honest I became. The more honest I was, the more vulnerable I became; the more vulnerable, the more insight I gained into God's character and my own heart. The walls came down in my heart of hearts and I found true freedom! I long for every reader to have this.

Decide now to answer all eleven questions.

You may write your answers in your head, on a napkin, or on a paper you'll throw away. But I recommend a journal just for your answers. If you answer the questions again and again at different junctures of your life — and if you find other questions Jesus is asking you — your own spiritual growth will be revealed through your entries. I think that's what floored me the most — how my answers changed in a few months' span.

A Few Other Notes

One of the most helpful books for this study is a *Harmony of the Gospels*. Having a Harmony alleviates all the flipping between pages of the four Gospels. I used *Harmony of the Gospels, Holman Christian Standard Bible* by Steven L. Cox and Kendall H. Easley. Unfortunately, it is now out of print, yet any Harmony is worth the purchase. I used the Harmony as a textbook. You should see my copy. I have highlighted every question Jesus asked, and it is full of sticky notes and scribbled notations in the margins. My Harmony became my *Unlocking Belief* Bible.

Some may think it to be presumptuous or even preposterous to answer questions Jesus asked over two thousand years ago. I believe it to be a rare privilege. I am excited for you as you embark on this journey.

Suzanne Matthews
November 2016

The holy use of the question, in whatever circumstance or however asked, is to draw me to Christ, so that I can begin to know Him, and, as a side note, gain insight into myself. The questions are to show me, Jesus. His questions show me, me. ⚷

CHAPTER 1

Why the Question

You said, 'Listen now, and I will speak;
I will question you, and you shall answer me.'
My ears had heard of you
but now my eyes have seen you.

- GOD'S SERVANT, JOB[1] -

ebster's Dictionary defines the word "question" as both noun and verb. As a noun, "question" means "a sentence worded or expressed so as to elicit information". As a verb, "question" means "to ask questions of (someone), especially in an official context".

Jesus asked questions. A lot of them. Hundreds are recorded in Scripture; there is no way of knowing the number unrecorded. Jesus Christ, the world's greatest communicator, used the question as a primary tool of communication. He asked rhetorical questions, questions to open a conversation and questions followed by illustration. He answered a question with a question, many questions He did not answer at all, and He often refrained from asking the obvious question. He asked questions of the Pharisees, the disciples, friends, specific individuals and general crowds. In direct contrast, not one question is spoken to Satan at His temptation, and His questions are completely absent in the Book of Revelation.

Did Jesus use the art of questioning to elicit information? Was His questioning used in an official context? Yes, and yes. The question for us is this: Why did Jesus use the question as His significant communication tool? Omniscient and All Knowing, He knew every answer.

An answer lies in the Book of Job. Through the briefest review of the Book of Job, we find in the first two chapters an introduction to the man God called — his servant, Job. We discover, through an exchange between God and Satan, that Job is to be tested. Job's testing results in the loss of children, property, and his own health. Even by today's standards, Job's tragedy and loss is horrific. The bulk of the book (chapters 3-37) relays the terrible anguish of Job, and recounts the words of Job's three friends, cursing the circumstances of Job's testing. God is silent until chapter 38, when He speaks.

> *Then the Lord answered Job out of the storm. He said: "Who is this that darkens my counsel with words without knowledge? Brace yourself like a man and I will question you, and you shall answer me." Job 38:1-3*

God begins to question Job, one question after another, profound questions of creation and the ways of the earth. Does Job know how God laid the earth's foundations, or where He fixed the boundaries of the sea? Has Job viewed the vast storehouses of snow and hail, or discovered the secrets of mountain goats, storks, and hawks? Questions unanswerable, except to the Creator.

When Job manages to speak, he says he has no answer to God, admitting his unworthiness and inability to answer such questions. God continues to question Job regarding His power, mentioning the terrifying behemoth and leviathan, beasts that even today we have no understanding of their identity. At the end of God's questioning, Job replies surely some of the most humble and repentant words every uttered.

> *"I know that you can do all things; no plan of yours can be thwarted. You asked, 'Who is this that obscures my counsel without knowledge?' Surely I spoke of things I did not understand, things too wonderful for me to know. You said, 'Listen now, and I will speak; I will question you, and you shall answer me.' My ears had heard of you but now my eyes have seen you. Therefore I despise myself and repent in dust and ashes." Job 42:2-6*

God's questions open our eyes to God
and reveal our hearts to ourselves.

Were God's questions to Job in an official context? Yes. Job rightly answered The God of all creation, the Sovereign. Did God's questions to Job elicit information? Yes. But *not* the information God needed; information that the one being questioned needed — information *Job* needed.

As much as we wish to know ourselves or think we do know ourselves, apart from God, we can be deceived by our own hearts. *The heart is deceitful above all things and beyond cure. Who can understand it?*[2] Have you ever been confused by your own heart? I have. Only God understands our hearts. *Man looks at the outward appearance, but the Lord looks at the heart.*[3] God, our Creator, knows our hearts inside and out, the good and the ugly. He sees what we cannot see. He sees the evil we hide; He sees the good of which we are unaware. Only God has an accurate view of our heart, and in spite of our heart's condition, God loves us. It is His desire to give us *a new heart*. So, like Job, as we glimpse the reality of our hearts, our mouths close, our eyes focus on God's character, and our trust in ourselves diminishes.

The Art of Asking Questions

Where did Jesus learn His questioning skills? Jesus was asking questions, deep questions, in His boyhood. His first recorded question is in *Luke 2:49*. Jesus was twelve years old and mistakenly left in Jerusalem after the feast of the Passover. Mary and Joseph returned to Jerusalem and searched for three days. When found in the temple courts, *asking and answering questions*, Jesus asks his mother:

> *Why were you searching for me? Didn't you know I had to be in my Father's house?*

As with the Son, also with the Father. We barely get our Bibles open to find that God's first question to man comes in the first chapters of God's recorded words to man. *Genesis 1:28* reveals those first recorded words. There are no questions.

> *God blessed them and said to them, "Be fruitful and increase in number; fill the earth and subdue it. Rule over the fish of the sea and the birds of the air and over every living creature that moves on the ground."*

In *Genesis 2:15-17* God explains death to man. There are no questions.

> *The Lord God took the man and put him in the Garden of Eden to work it and take care of it. And the Lord God commanded the man, "You are free to eat from any tree in the garden; but you must not eat from the tree of the knowledge of good and evil, for when you eat of it you will surely die."*

God's first words to man held *no question*. The turning point comes in *Genesis 3:9*. Adam and Eve have eaten from the forbidden fruit and upon hearing the sound of God in the garden, they hid.

> *But the Lord God called to the man, "Where are you?"*

Think on this

God's first *question* was to *fallen* man.

The fall of man brought the first question from God. Charles Spurgeon preached a sermon on this topic titled, *God's First Words to the First Sinner* [4]:

> "The sinner comes not to God; God comes to him. It is not, 'My God, where are You?' But the first cry is the voice of Grace, 'Sinner where are you?' God comes to man; man seeks not his God.

> "And now hear the voice of God as He cries, 'Adam, where are you?' Oh, there were two Truths of God in that short sentence! It showed

that Adam was lost, or God would not have needed to ask him where he was. Until we have lost a thing, we need not inquire about it. But when God said, 'Adam, where are you?' it was the voice of a shepherd inquiring for his lost sheep. Or better still, the cry of a loving parent asking for his child that has run away from him, 'Where are you?'"

Think on this

The art of asking questions, the grace in asking a question — Jesus shared with His Father.

The questions asked by our Lord are not for His benefit, or to give Him knowledge, or bring Him to further understanding. He needs no further benefit, counsel, knowledge, or understanding.

The holy use of the question, in whatever circumstance or however asked, is to draw me to Christ, so that I can begin to know Him, and, as a side note, gain insight into myself. The questions are to show me, Jesus. His questions show me, me.

Apart from God I cannot know myself. I want to, I think I do. Yet without God, I am greatly misled and mistaken. I can find me — I can find God — by bracing myself as Job did, facing the One who questions, and attempting to answer.

Following Jesus

From this point forward, our study will track Jesus' ministry in chronological order. We begin at a remote location near Bethany, Judea, at the Jordan River. Long streams of people walked the dusty roads to find John the Baptist preaching and baptizing. In the mix, dubious priests and Levites from Jerusalem came to watch and called out their questions. *"Who are you? Give us an answer to take back to those who sent us. What do you say about yourself?"* The Baptist's response was clear. *"I am not the Christ. I am the voice of one calling in the desert, 'Make straight the way for the Lord.'"*[5]

After spending forty days in the Judean desert being tempted by Satan, Jesus appeared at the Jordan River. In accordance with the will of His Father, Jesus desired to be baptized by John. John was hesitant; Jesus gently insistent. After Jesus' baptism, heaven opened to confirm the Father's pleasure with His Son.

The next day, Jesus again walked to the Jordan. John the Baptist noticed Him, and speaking to two of his own disciples, said, *Look, the Lamb of God!* As the two disciples began to follow, Jesus turned to them and asked,

---

Pivotal Question #1

What are you looking for?

John 1:38

Two thousand years after Jesus first appeared, these questions still hang in the air, awaiting our answers. Most of his questions were never answered. Indeed most of them have been deliberately ignored.

- JOHN DEAR [7] -

This is hard.

- AN EXCERPT FROM MY JOURNAL [8] -

Pivotal Question #1

What are you looking for?

Read the surrounding verses in *John 1:19-51.*

Jot down some of the facts regarding the few days following Jesus' baptism by John the Baptist. Who was Jesus speaking to when He asked this pivotal question? Where was He? How did the two disciples respond?

If Jesus asked you this question today, how would you respond to Him?

Answer it, journal it. Take all the time you need. This is, and will be each week, the most important element of our study. In your journal, start, come back to it, add to it, revise it; just answer it.

It does not have to be long, but it does need to reflect where you are at the moment. You will never be asked to unwillingly share your writings. This is between you and Christ.

To glean a little more understanding into the very first few days of Jesus' ministry, read *John 1:40-51.* What stands out to you? There are no right answers; just write what strikes you as interesting, unusual, or of note.

Week 1 Study Guide

Revisit: Asking Questions

1. Before we begin to look at the variety of Jesus' questions, I want us to think a little bit more about asking questions. Why does Jesus ask so many questions when He fully knows the answers?

2. Try to read between the lines and hear the tone and inflection in His voice. Two examples are especially good for this: Jesus' exchange with Nicodemus and then with the Samaritan woman. Read both passages: *John 2:23 – 3:21* and *John 4:5-42*.

[Note: in the NIV Jesus asks the Samaritan woman, "Will you give me a drink?"]

Write down the things you notice about each conversation.

3. What are things you have noticed regarding the speaking style of the people close to you? Think of a family member, your child, or a good friend. Give as many examples as possible of how you know those close to you through their words and their voices.

4. Somewhere in your journal, begin to chart your own questions. Do you ask questions? What kinds of questions do you ask? When do you ask questions?

Where was Jesus?

As we track Jesus' ministry chronologically, I would like to keep up with where He is geographically.

5. Where was Jesus:

- When He was baptized?

- When He called his first disciples?

- When He turned water into wine?

- When He spoke with Nicodemus?

- When He met the Samaritan woman?

6. Where was He headed?

Jesus' Early Ministry

The rest of our study this week will focus on getting a comprehensive view of Jesus' early ministry. The questions He asked were often rhetorical or closed teaching questions. The manner in which He asked a question changed, depending to whom He was speaking.

6. Begin to highlight Jesus' questions while skimming the Scriptures we are not studying in depth. Review these three sections of Scripture and make brief notes of your thoughts and observations:

- *John 5:1-47* — Jesus' Third Sign: Healing the Sick

- *Matthew 5-7* and *Luke 6* — The Sermon on the Mount

- *Luke 7:36-50* — Much Forgiveness, Much Love

7. If you are a hands-on learner as I am, placing fingers on a map brings knowledge of the location of Jesus, but more importantly offers insight to His God-directed steps. Using a map of Israel during Jesus' time, find these three places:

- John the Baptist was baptizing at the Jordan river slightly northeast from Bethany

- Judea and Jerusalem

- Find Galilee and trace the fastest route from Judea to Galilee.

I do not want you to ever doubt that Jesus would take the hard route, come into the defiled place, enter hostility and heartbreak, for one woman — you. ⎯⎯⚷

CHAPTER 2

Home to Galilee

He is not a man like me that I might answer him,
that we might confront each other in court.
If only there were someone to arbitrate between us,
to lay his hand on us both.

- GOD'S SERVANT, JOB[1] -

I am a hands-on learner. I think with my fingers. I have been pouring over a map of Jesus' travel routes. As my fingers trace His journeys I begin to feel "place". There is something in His very place at a particular time of ministry that is foundational to the story. Especially this story.

Jesus has entered year one of His ministry. He spent time traveling through the Judean countryside with the first of His disciples. When Herod locked up John the Baptist in prison, Jesus heard of the imprisonment and returned to Galilee. Matthew's Gospel says, *He **withdrew** into Galilee*[2]; Luke says, *Jesus returned to Galilee **in the power of the Spirit.***[3] Both writers make sure we know that these particular steps were especially directed by God. *He withdrew* denotes Galilee as a safe place for Jesus, a place where He would spend a great deal of time away from the rumor and rejection found in Jerusalem. Galilee was home. Galilee would become a place of popularity and companionship, a place where He drew close to the people, touched the crowds, healed, and taught and lived. Aptly named His great Galilean ministry, the months in the north held close conversations, intimate healings, and widespread teachings to large followings. It would not be so later in His ministry. This was His time with the people.

Tracing the route from Judea to Galilee, there is no way to miss that the fastest route goes directly north through Samaria. Samaritans had a long divisive history with Judeans. Samaritans were detested by Jews, and in revolt had developed their own version of the law, their own mountain, their own temple for worship The hatred that began generations prior, still ran deep in Jesus' day. To a strict Jew, it was defiling even to walk on Samaritan ground. So, in order to avoid uncleanness, they took the longer route.

Yet *John 4:4* says Jesus *had to* travel to Samaria. Why? To what purpose? The words "had to" translate as "to be necessary, a divine necessity." [4] As Jesus withdrew to the homeland of Galilee, God had Him take a detour of eternal significance. It was much more than being the shortest route; the route was necessary.

Think on this

Jesus went to Samaria for one woman.

So he came to a town in Samaria called Sychar, near the plot of ground Jacob had given to his son Joseph. Jacob's well was there, and Jesus, tired as he was from the journey, sat down by the well. It was about noon.

When a Samaritan woman came to draw water, Jesus said to her, "Will you give me a drink?" (His disciples had gone into the town to buy food.) The Samaritan woman said to him, "You are a Jew and I am a Samaritan woman. How can you ask me for a drink?" (For Jews do not associate with Samaritans.)

Jesus answered her, "If you knew the gift of God and who it is that asks you for a drink, you would have asked him and he would have given you living water."

"Sir," the woman said, "you have nothing to draw with and the well is deep. Where can you get this living water? Are you greater than our father Jacob, who gave us the well and drank from it himself, as did also his sons and his livestock?"

Jesus answered, "Everyone who drinks this water will be thirsty again, but whoever drinks the water I give them will never thirst. Indeed, the water I give them will become in them a spring of water welling up to eternal life."

The woman said to him, "Sir, give me this water so that I won't get thirsty and have to keep coming here to draw water."

He told her, "Go, call your husband and come back."

"I have no husband," she replied.

Jesus said to her, "You are right when you say you have no husband. The fact is, you have had five husbands, and the man you now have is not your husband. What you have just said is quite true."

"Sir," the woman said, "I can see that you are a prophet. Our ancestors worshiped on this mountain, but you Jews claim that the place where we must worship is in Jerusalem."

"Woman," Jesus replied, "believe me, a time is coming when you will worship the Father neither on this mountain nor in

Jerusalem. You Samaritans worship what you do not know; we worship what we do know, for salvation is from the Jews. Yet a time is coming and has now come when the true worshipers will worship the Father in the Spirit and in truth, for they are the kind of worshipers the Father seeks. God is spirit, and his worshipers must worship in the Spirit and in truth."

The woman said, "I know that Messiah" (called Christ) "is coming. When he comes, he will explain everything to us."

Then Jesus declared, "I, the one speaking to you—I am he."

John 4:5-26

Who was this woman, the one for whom Jesus *had* to go to meet? She was a Samaritan, by her race; a Jew would have viewed her as defiled. She was alone, coming to get water in the heat of the day. Scholars differ as to whether the Samaritan woman came to the well in the heat of the day or at the end of the day. By either interpretation, noon or six, the place was empty.

The place was deserted. Where were all the other women? Right. The well was a natural gathering spot, a Starbucks of our day, and women walked there in the early morning hours before the heat of the day. At noon or six, they were at home, cooking and caring for their families. Going at that time, this Samaritan woman was assured to be alone.

She had been married five times. She was living with another man, not married to him. I expect she was the butt of much gossip, that lively conversations hushed when she walked near. Can you imagine her inner shame, her humiliation? Dismayed at seeing a man at the well, a Jewish man, she approached, surely feeling if she ignored him she would be invisible. I bet she was good at making herself invisible.

Jesus asks *only one* question. *Will you give me a drink?* A Jewish man speaking to a Samaritan woman was an astonishing break with culture. She is first surprised, then interested. He tells her that He is the giver of eternal water, the kind of water that she will never again have to seek. She wants that. Badly. Anything, not to have to come back to this well everyday. Jesus begins speaking in double meanings. He speaks of the spiritual; she interprets the physical. She hears Him through the lens of her life.

Even though their conversation is on two different levels, trust begins to grow. He makes a statement; she responds. When Jesus delivers the searing words, *Go, call your husband*, amazingly, she did not lie. How easy it would have been to squirm, to back off, to mumble something and be done. Yet, she is honest. Not only honest, she is vulnerable. She leans in to hear what He is saying, and meaning. She yearns for His refreshing, appealing water.

This is not a question and answer exchange. The point is not that Jesus only asked her one question, that there were no further questions after the first one. Or that Jesus refrained from asking her the whereabouts of her friends, details of her circumstances, if she had a husband, or how many husbands she had previously. *Why?*

Because she *believed* Him. It may have only been the tiniest seed of belief, but Jesus recognized belief when He saw it. And He responded to it.

Think on this

Jesus reveals to the Samaritan woman who He is.

Her *belief* opened the door for Jesus to reveal Himself. Everywhere He went, and with everyone, Jesus held tightly to His identity until the timing to reveal Himself was perfect. With her, He openly, tenderly, stated universe shattering words, *I am He.* Those words *I am* were the words God told Moses regarding His Name, *"This is what you are to say to the Israelites: 'I AM has sent me to you.'"* [5] Those words, *I am He*, Jesus spoke to soldiers in Gethsemane and tough military men fell to the ground.[6] How ironic that in Samaria, with a woman, Jesus found a safe person. And she found the Christ, the Great I Am, the Giver of Eternal Life, the Well of Eternal Water.

Do we recognize this same gift when it appears in our lives? The gift of safe people?

A safe person in your life is the person you can reveal yourself to, *the worst or the best*, and know they love you. We recognize safe people not with our heads, but with our hearts. Our gut tells us when someone is safe. Subconsciously, we know.

I discovered my safe people at a time when I was hurting so badly, the only way I knew to act was awful. I actively set out to ruin every relationship I valued. I could not imagine being able to stand me; I could not stand me. A wise counselor came to my aid and explained safe people. I recognized that my safe people, *the ones I loved the most*, were being battered and bruised *by me*. Later, I came to know that just as we have safe people, we are safe people to some. We get bruised and beaten up by the hurting one who subconsciously knows we will still love and not leave. If you are thinking right now of who is safe to you and to whom you are safe, please allow me to affirm you, give you a big pat on the back, and mention, that being someone's safe person sometimes feels like being a punching bag. And as encouragement, let me say it is a compliment to you, although it may feel like a backhanded one, to be considered safe to another. You are a person of great value to the one who considers you safe.

Jesus knows who is safe. Inherently, we do too.

Jesus is our safest person.

I know who my safe people are. I know a few who consider me to be their safe person. Yet my world was rocked when I realized Jesus is the safest of all. So safe, so free, was the Samaritan woman that she forgot her water jar and ran to town confessing to even the ones who had shamed her, *Come, see a man who told me everything I ever did! Could this be the Messiah?*[7] Her seed of belief sprouted, and a wave of faith began that day in Samaria.

All for One

I love that Jesus went personally into hostile territory to rescue one woman. Another time in scripture He did almost the same thing — He sent an army in for one person.

In the beginning chapters of Joshua, Jesus instructed Joshua how to enter the most fortified city of the day, Jericho. Joshua's spies did their homework well, and relayed detailed information to Joshua, their general. However vital the information, it was not necessary in the end. God rewarded their obedience, miraculously brought down the thick walls, and Joshua's men simply walked over rubble to enter the famed city.[8]

And once in? Joshua was sent into Jericho for one woman. Rahab. God's men went into Jericho to save Rahab and her family. And once saved? Rahab married into the Hebrew family and became one of only four women recorded by name in Matthew's lineage of Jesus.[9]

> I do not want you to ever doubt that Jesus would take the hard route, come into the defiled place, enter hostility and heartbreak, for one woman — you.

Jesus found me, or rather I found Him, in a lonely place my junior year in college. Through some hard family upheavals, my flimsy safety net was pulled out from under me, and I floundered. God entered the uncertainty of my life through a friend who delivered a word of Truth, and my heart opened wide to receive Christ. Jesus is still in the business of going to unlikely, unpopular, unforgiving, overlooked places, to gather one woman's heart. Yours. And mine.

Back to Nazareth

Jesus left the safety of Samaria and entered Galilee, familiar territory near home. It was a time of great acclaim with the people. Crowds flocked to Jesus, eager to hear His voice, feel His touch, listen to His teaching. Yet from the beginning, controversy surrounded Him. It was in His hometown of Nazareth where he was rejected, and the plot to end His life took root. In Nazareth no question from Jesus is recorded. Later, on a trip to Jerusalem,

Jesus asks an invalid, *Do you want to get well?* It is when Jesus commanded the man on the Sabbath, *Pick up your mat and walk*, that hatred went to seed and its thick roots would entangle Him until His last days.[10]

Jesus traveled through Galilee miles and days, preaching the most well-known teachings in history, the Sermon on the Mount. His words became guarded; He spoke through parables, using intensely personal, but rhetorical, questions. The countryside was abuzz with interest, conversations everywhere questioned the meaning in His words. Exhausted and in need of sleep, Jesus pulled away with His disciples. They boarded a fishing vessel on the Sea of Galilee, known for its fierce, sudden storms. Jesus was sleeping in the stern of the boat when a quick, ferocious storm erupted. Fearing death, the terrified disciples woke Jesus.

With the voice of authority, the Creator subdued creation. As the sea turned to glass, Jesus asked the disciples two questions. They never answered.

Pivotal Question #2

Why are you fearful?

Matthew 8:26; Mark 4:40

Pivotal Question #3

Do you still have no faith?

Luke 8:25

She could tell he was a Jew by his dress. She was silent. She wasn't about to speak to him! While she was getting ready to lower her bucket into the well, however, Jesus made a request.

He asked for a drink.

This is always the way it is in the spiritual realm. Jesus comes to us first. If we were left to ourselves, we would leave him sitting on the edge of the well forever. But he does not leave us to ourselves. Instead he comes to us. He asks the first question. He initiates the conversation.

He uses all devices to break through to our hearts.

-JAMES MONTGOMERY BOICE [11]-

Am I fearful Lord Jesus?

Just three weeks ago, when Ben's heart stopped, I faintly felt fear grip my heart. Then you took over and there was no room for fear. A few days later, when all the Bible study was fasting for eight days, I fasted from fear. You took away the fear and it has stayed far from my thoughts, with the exception of that one night, when I was completely overwhelmed by the thoughts of the future — our future.

You taught me much of fear. It is the first reaction, a deep ingrained human response. It is debilitating. It squelches faith. I once heard that fear and faith cannot sit on the same bench. How I have seen that to be true in my own private thought life.

While fasting from fear, I remembered how you taught me four months ago that You value belief. Through all of this I have put believing you at the forefront of my thoughts.

With belief, there is little room for fear.

-AN EXCERPT FROM MY JOURNAL [12]-

Why are you fearful?

Matthew 8:26; Mark 4:40

Do you still have no faith?

Luke 8:25

Read all three passages: *Mark 4:35-41; Matthew 8:18-19, 23-27;* and *Luke 8:22-25.* Look up *Mark 4:40* in several other translations (for instance, the *New International Version*, *English Standard Version* and *The Message*).

The Bible has no mention if or how any of the disciples in the boat answered Jesus.

If Jesus asked you these questions today, how would you respond to Him?

Let the questions sit in your heart and mind for a few days. Pray over them. With pen and journal, take some time to answer the questions by journaling your thoughts. Often my thoughts come to me with clarity, and even new insights, when I begin to write them down.

Jesus' questions are not for the fainthearted. They cause us to think deeply and often bring up painful memories. Through His questions, Jesus gently pulls our doubts right to the forefront of our hearts, then pushes us along to further trust in His character.

This is, and will be each week, the most important element of our study. **If we do not answer the questions, then our study becomes simply a chronological reflection of Jesus' ministry.** In your journal, start, come back to it, add to it, revise it; just begin to answer the question. After writing my answer to the first question, I left several pages blank in my journal, hoping and trusting Jesus would show me a fuller answer in days to come.

You will never be asked to unwillingly share your writings. This is between you and Christ.

Week 2 Study Guide

As we continue studying Jesus' ministry, skim through Scripture passages that we will not study in depth. Take note of every question Jesus asked. Each time you see a change in location, highlight the name of the town or region. Stay close to your map, charting His travels.

Word of Jesus spread like wildfire and the crowds increased in number. All twelve of Jesus' disciples were selected. Put yourself in the place of the disciples; listen to what they are hearing, see what they are watching, reflect upon what they ask of Jesus and what they refrain from asking. In this lesson we are going to attempt to draw close enough to Jesus to sense His emotions through His words and the specific wording of the Gospel writer's phrases.

Revisit: Back to Nazareth

1. Read *Matthew 13:54-58* and *Mark 6:1-6a.*

   - Where was Jesus? Who was with Him?

   - What were the questions asked about Him?

   - Why was Jesus unable to do many miracles?

   - In *Mark 6* what amazed Jesus?

2. Revisit *Matthew 8:5-13* and *Luke 7:1-10.*

   - Where was Jesus? Who approached Jesus and what was asked of Jesus?

   - In *Matthew 8:10* and *Luke 7:9* what amazed Jesus?

   The word "amazed" may be translated, "astonished" or "marveled". The two occasions mentioned in questions one and two above are the two times in the New Testament when Jesus was actually described as *astonished*. The *only* two times.

3. What are your thoughts regarding what caused Jesus to be astonished?

4. Using your own life circumstances, how would you describe your faith and your unbelief?

The Heart of the Teacher

Jesus' ministry was advancing, the crowds were increasing, the dialog was deepening. Jesus then decided to send out His disciples in pairs to nearby towns to preach and heal.

5. Read *Matthew 9:35 – 11:1*.

   • To whom were they to go? What were Jesus' instructions?

   • How had they been previously prepared? What were they to expect?

6. From *Matthew 14:1-12*, what caused the disciples to return to Jesus?

7. Read *Matthew 14:31-23; Mark 6:30-46; Luke 9:10-17;* and *John 6:1-15*.

   • After Jesus heard of the death of John the Baptist, what did He do?

   • What was His intention? What actually happened?

8. After the crowds were fed, what did Jesus do? Why?

9. Trace back through the last few days in Jesus' life. If you had to guess, what was on His heart and what might be included in His prayers to His Father?

10. Do you sense a shift in His focus? If so, what is it?

11. Wrapping up this section, once again scribes and Pharisees came from Jerusalem for Jesus. Read *Mark 7:1-30*.

    • In verse 18, what question does Jesus ask? To whom?

    • In your opinion, what was Jesus' tone of voice and His emotions?

    • What does *Mark 7:24-30* say about Jesus?

12. After reading *Mark 8:10-12*, how do you picture Jesus?

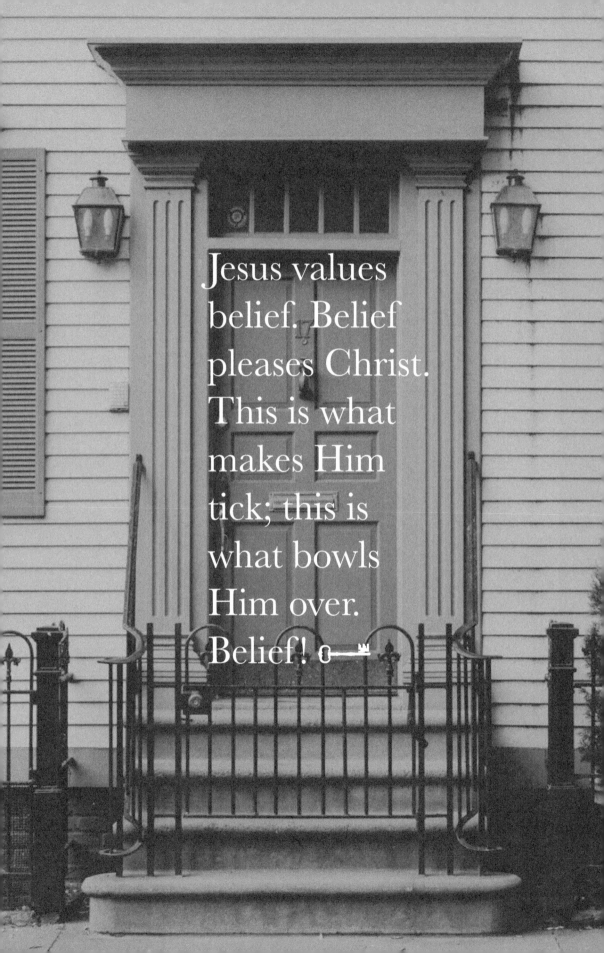

Jesus values belief. Belief pleases Christ. This is what makes Him tick; this is what bowls Him over. Belief! ⚷

CHAPTER 3

Growing Fame and Growing Opposition

Consequently, faith comes from hearing the message, and the message is heard through the word of Christ.

-PAUL, A SERVANT OF CHRIST JESUS[1]-

After Jesus calmed the Sea of Galilee and after the disciples recovered from their death grip of fear, their first response was, *Who can this be?*[2], the question that began to replace all previous questions. The question the disciples would ask again and again. Jesus was speaking plainly. Especially to them.

Their boat arrived in Gentile territory. No sooner had they landed, a demon possessed man ran from the tombs and knelt before Jesus, crying, *What do you have to do with me, Jesus, Son of the Most High God?* Jesus did not ask, "Who are you?" He asked, *What is your Name?* Whereas many have sidetracked His questions, the demon possessed man truthfully answered Jesus, *My name is Legion, because we are many.*[3] A Roman legion consisted of six thousand soldiers.

This is not the first time a demon spoke with no doubt, the identity of Jesus. The demon called Jesus by His Name, *Son of the Most High God.*

Up until this point in His ministry, Jesus has revealed only once His true identity — to the Samaritan woman. Remember He said to her, *I Am He*.

This is a good time to stop for a moment and reflect on the Names of Christ, on the Names of God. *Names*, plural. In this passage, a demon possessed man revealed one Name of Christ. In the previous chapter, we discovered the Name God spoke for Himself at the burning bush to Moses, *I Am*.

God continued with Moses:

> *This is what you're to say to the Israelites: "God, the God of your fathers, the God of Abraham, the God of Isaac, and the God of Jacob sent me to you." This has always been my name, and this is how I always will be known.*[1]

I AM — the Name that transcends all time and space. The name that assures us our God is past, present, future, eternal, infinite. *I AM* was the name so hallowed by the Israelites, it could not be breathed. They created a code word — YAHWEH — *Jehovah*.

Names are important. Just think of the thought and prayer, the time spent researching, or trying out names for our children before they are born. Our given name may be the one on our birth certificates, but we are known by several names, not just one. We have our legal name, a nickname, a term of endearment, the name often assigned by our coworkers, or our name to close friends. We call ourselves names, and most of us have been called not-so-nice names by others. One singular name does not identify who we are. We are a combination of all our names. We spend a lifetime making a name, growing into a name, or trying to undo a name. A name. It is quite significant to who we are and who we want to be.

When others know us very well, they know us by many of our names. I know my friend by her legal name, what her friends call her, what her children call her, even the grandmother name she has chosen for herself. My favorite name is my grandmother name, *Zannie*. I hope my grandchildren know Zannie to be loving and generous, loyal, firm, and a barrel of fun. As they grow up, I hope they will always know Zannie loves them and Zannie loves God. As I learn to be a grandmother, I am growing into my name, *Zannie*.

Recently my four-year-old granddaughter was at Disney World with her parents and siblings. Hot from the sun and tired from walking, she noticed at several kiosks, plastic water bottles connected to a battery operated fan; they blew cool water on her face. They were expensive and she was told several times she could not have one. After hearing 'no' one too many times, in the middle of meltdown, she replied, "If Zannie was here she would give me umpteen dollars for one!" Caroline believed I would save the day. I want Zannie to be the one who will save the day!

Just as others come to know us by our names, we come to know God by His names. The Godhead has over six hundred names in Scripture, from Genesis to Revelation. The Person of Jesus Christ, His very character, is found in *all* His names. We begin to know Jesus intimately by identifying with His names in Scripture. When we are distraught, we come to know Him as Comforter; when we need advice, we know Him as Wonderful Counselor; when we need strength, He is our Rock. There is a name for every need.

Think on this

If we wish to know God,
we begin to know His Son by name.

Believing He Can

Wouldn't you love to be a fly on the deck of the disciples' fishing boat, and watch their expressions, hear their conversations? A lot was happening on the Sea of Galilee. With their own eyes, they saw Jesus calm the sea. In the Gerasenes, with their own ears, they listened as Jesus allowed a legion of demons to enter a herd of swine, and watched while the herd went over a steep bank and drowned in the lake. The people of the region begged Jesus and His disciples to leave. It must have been a hushed group of twelve boarding the boat. As they crossed the Sea of Galilee again, surely they noticed as far as they could see, people flocking to the shoreline in hopes to glimpse the Teacher.

As soon as they landed they were met by Jairus, the synagogue leader. Nearby, Jairus' daughter was dying. With no time to wait, Jairus begged Jesus to come to the bedside of his daughter. While Jesus was making His way through the thick throng of people, news came that the little daughter had already died. When Jesus overheard the pronouncement, He turned to Jairus and said, *Don't be afraid. Only believe.* Arriving at the house, Jesus took only the parents, with Peter, James, and John into the child's room, lay His hands on her, and spoke words of life. She got up, was given food, and Jesus commanded silence to her parents and the three disciples, that no one should know of this event.[5]

Jesus left Jairus' house and was followed by two blind men shouting for mercy, begging for their sight. Jesus said to them, *Do you believe that I can do this?* They answered, *Yes, Lord.* Jesus touched their eyes, said, *Let it be done to you according to your faith!* and their eyes were opened.[6]

*Don't be afraid, only **believe**. Do you **believe** that I can do this?* These words flooded my heart on July 25, 2014. Sitting in the den with my husband, getting ready to go to his dental appointment, I suddenly heard a sucking, wheezing sound. I turned my head to Ben, and at one glance I knew something was horribly wrong — life threatening. Gasping for breath and unresponsive, I know now that Ben was experiencing sudden cardiac arrest. I called 911 and time slowed; I felt the minutes dragging through quicksand. Simultaneously, time zoomed in fast-forward; all our married years rolled out before me. I begged God for Ben's life. No, to be perfectly truthful, I first *bargained* with God. I hate to admit it, but it is true. My split-second conversation with God went something like this: "I will do anything you ask of me if you will save him, God. No! Forgive me God, I do not mean to bargain with You. You are God! You say, *Come now, let us reason together*[7], so I am laying out my reasons to you, God. Surely we are not finished yet, our life together can't be over yet. It went so fast." Still to this day I have hyper-memory of the following moments and hours. Overall, I kept thinking, "Don't think, just believe. Believe. Believe. And I remembered Jesus said, *Do you believe that I can do this?*

Two months earlier, I had taught *Unlocking Belief* to the first pilot group, and the lesson you are now reading was the lesson that seared itself into my heart and mind. I knew I believed *in* Jesus, but really, how strong was my belief? In fact, just what did I truly believe *about* Jesus?

In Scripture there are two, *and only two*, earthly instances which amazed and astonished Jesus. The first is when Jesus, while traveling through Galilee, was approached by *Jewish* elders on behalf of a *Roman* centurion. That would be enough to get our attention, but the elders spoke glowing words of the Roman centurion, and told Jesus the centurion's beloved servant was dying. Further, the centurion sent word that Jesus need not come to his home; he believed Jesus had the authority to simply say the word, and his slave would be healed. *Jesus heard this and was* **amazed** *(emphasis mine) at him, and turning to the crowd following him, he said, "I tell you, I have not found so great a faith even in Israel!"* [8] When the elders and friends returned to the centurion's home, the slave was found healthy. The word "amazed" comes from the Greek root word *thaumazo*, meaning "to look closely at, to wonder, have in admiration, to marvel." [9] This is the first instance when *thaumazo* is used in the Bible regarding Jesus.

The second time *thaumazo* appears, Jesus was teaching in the synagogue in His hometown, Nazareth. People began to question His wisdom, question the facts surrounding the many miraculous healings throughout Galilee. They remembered He was the carpenter, Mary's son, and they questioned how someone local could be so learned. Mark says they were *offended*. Jesus was unable to perform many miracles in Nazareth. *He was* **amazed** *(emphasis mine) at their unbelief.* [10]

This word, *thaumazo*, is used only twice in reference to Jesus. Two times Jesus was amazed at something, marveled at someone, was truly astonished. Belief in one instance; unbelief in the other.

 Jesus values belief. Belief pleases Christ. This is what makes Him tick; this is what bowls Him over. *Belief!*

The people you know really well, you know what gets to them, what triggers makes them laugh or cry, what thrills or upsets them. You know their back story and how it figures in to who they are. You know what makes them tick. These two passages provide a monumental hint at what brings Jesus joy, or what hurts His heart. It is what He is amazed by — belief and unbelief.

If we want to know Jesus, know what bowls Him over.
What astonishes the Son of God? It is belief.

But, belief in *what*?

Jesus never asked the two blind men, "Do you believe I will do this?" His question was, *Do you believe that I can do this?* Believing Jesus *can* is vastly different from believing Jesus *will*. Jesus asks us to believe He *can*.

I hung on to one word for days, *believe*. I began to recount to myself over and over the things I do believe. I believe God created heaven and earth. I believe Jesus is the one and only Son of God, the Way to eternal life. I believe Jesus was indeed human, came to earth, and died on the cross for my sins. I believe the cross really happened. I believe God brought Jesus back to life, and now He is fully alive. I believe the Bible is the Word of God and divinely inspired. I believe I belong to Jesus. I believe He loves me. I believe He will never leave or forsake me.

Belief is believing that *He can*, not necessarily that *He will*. I was giving my best shot at believing Jesus *could* do it, not necessarily that He *would*; believing whatever He did would be good, believing He had my back, believing He had Ben. Four days later, God gave my husband back to us. He gained consciousness, had no heart or brain damage. God gave us a living miracle. Do I believe that my belief saved my husband? Oh, no. Unequivocally, no. God's saving Ben was God's will at work in Ben. God's work in me was my journey of belief: learning that even one minuscule speck of true belief was enough to carry *me* through. I learned how important it is to simply believe in Jesus. *The work of God is this: to believe in the one he has sent.*[11]

Believing Through Doubt

Still the crowds, the pressure, the people, the need. After Jesus heard that John the Baptist had been killed by Herod, in His grief He withdrew to Bethsaida. He was met by thousands. If it had been me, I would have wanted to hide, or slip away unnoticed. Surely some of the disciples, maybe even Jesus, wished to get back on the boat. The Bible says He had compassion on them. He loved them. So he nourished them. Body and soul. Later He explained, revealing another name, *I am the Bread of Life. No one who comes to me will ever be hungry, and no one who believes in me will ever be thirsty again.*[12]

It is believed over 25,000 people were fed that day, marking the end of Jesus' second full year of ministry. And after? Did He find a place to collapse in sheer exhaustion? No. He sent the disciples in the boat ahead of Him, and He went to a mountaintop to pray. What He needed most was time with His Father. I have often wondered if Jesus looked out over the sea and saw the little boat full of His friends struggling against the wind. This time Jesus walked out on the raging sea, and the disciples believed they were seeing a ghost. He assured them, *Have courage! It is I. Don't be afraid.* Peter wanted to walk to Jesus, but the strength of the wind and sea gave him doubt and fear. Jesus grasped Peter and said, *O you of little faith, why did you doubt?*[13]

If we believe, why do we doubt? When we doubt, does it mean we do not believe? If we look closely at the biblical accounts, there is a strong connection between faith and fear. Or rather, a disconnect. Yes, if we are to grow our faith, we must squarely face what causes our doubts. But the bigger question is, what causes our fears? I heard it said years ago, "Fear and faith cannot sit on the same bench; one will always kick the other off."

Think on this

Fear removes our faith. Fear causes unbelief.

Jesus finally had the much needed alone moment with his disciples to bring them further in their faith. He asked them, *Who do people say that the Son of Man is?* They replied various choices — Elijah, John the Baptist. *But you, He asked them, who do you say that I am?* No one answered his question, except for Peter. And Jesus changed Peter's name.[14]

Pivotal Question #4

Who do you say I am?

Matthew 16:13-15; Mark 4:27-20; Luke 9:18-21

At some point along our faith journey, Jesus turns to each one of us, as well, and asks us this same question. "Who do you say that I am?" Each one of us needs to spend time with this question. We can imagine the gentle eyes of Jesus looking at us, smiling with his usual loving kindness, and hoping for our faith and loving affirmation. But he knows too that we do not yet understand any of this, so he tries to draw us out, to lead us to the truth, to help us figure it out. The identity of Jesus then is at the heart of his story and our lives.

- JOHN DEAR[15]-

Pivotal Question #4

Who do you say I am?

Matthew 16:13-15; Mark 4:27-20; Luke 9:18-21

Read all three passages. In Jesus' day, who did the people say He was? In our day, who do people say Jesus is? Who do you believe him to be?

If Jesus asked you this question today, how would you respond to Him?

Answer the question in your journal after reading and completing this page.

I have realized the questions we are answering cannot be completed, or even begun, without prayer. Pray as the question sits in your heart before you begin to answer. Pray over your answer after you answer. Ask for wisdom and to be given a *gradual fuller understanding*, just as Jesus taught through the blind man in

Mark 8:22-26. I am convinced by my own answers that the more honest I am with God, the more He reveals Himself to me.

Jesus is safe. We do not need to sugar-coat our answers to Him. You will never be asked to unwillingly share your writings. This is between you and Christ.

Jesus, at the feeding of the five thousand, was at the end of His second full year of ministry. Our study picks up in the first six months of His third year of ministry.

First Prediction of Jesus' Death & Resurrection

Matthew 16:21-16, Mark 8:31-37, Luke 9:22-25

Scripture states, *from then on Jesus began to point out to His disciples that He must go to Jerusalem and suffer many things.* Jesus knew and clearly told of his upcoming death.

1. What is the preceding event that caused Jesus to begin predicting His suffering and death?

2. What words did Jesus use to describe his death?

3. How did Jesus refer to His resurrection?

Second Prediction of Jesus' Death

Matthew 17:22-23, Mark 9:30-32, Luke 9:43-45

4. Where were Jesus and the disciples and what key event had happened just prior to Jesus' second announcement of His coming death?

5. From the Mark passage, list each point in Jesus' statement to His disciples.

6. From all three passages, what was the reaction of the disciples?

7. What does the disciples' response teach you about their hearts and minds at the moment?

Feast of Tabernacles

Luke 9:51-56, John 7:10-52

This is the turning point in Jesus' ministry.

8. Read both passages, and using the study notes in your Bible or other resources, briefly explain the Feast of Tabernacles.

9. Why did Jesus go secretly to the Feast of Tabernacles?

10. What in these two passages points to a turning point in Jesus' ministry?

11. Reflecting on a turning point in your own life, what does Jesus' example teach you?

12. In the back of your journal, list the letters of the alphabet. Begin your own list of the Names of God by writing names you have learned thus far in our study. Jot the verse next to each name. Let me get you started:

A — Alpha and Omega, *Revelation 22:13*

B — Beloved Son, *Luke 3:22*

C — Creator of heaven and earth, *Genesis 14:2*

I read the Bible to listen. Sometimes I learn something of God's character, sometimes I read to study a passage, sometimes I flip my Bible open randomly and read for sheer comfort. While I read, I listen for God's voice. ⚷

CHAPTER 4

The Turning Point

I do believe! Help my unbelief.

- A FATHER OF A BOY[1] -

Driving the main route to my house I make two ninety-degree turns. As I approach each turn, I slow down. As I make the turn, I apply the brakes and I pay attention to oncoming traffic, vehicles behind me, and particularly, staying in my lane. Once through the turn, I speed up and head for home.

We are to the turning point in Jesus' ministry. Just as there are several steps in navigating the turns on my way home, the turning point of Jesus' ministry is not just one event. Three specific events — the Transfiguration, a conversation with a father, and the Feast of Tabernacles — chart the course and form the transition. Circumstances have changed, locations have changed, and the manner of Jesus' teaching is about to change. His words become stronger, more emphatic. He knows His time is limited; He has less than a year of earthly ministry.

To fully take in the turning point of Jesus' ministry, we will slow down to approach the turn, pay careful attention while making the turn, then speed up and set off in a totally different direction as we head home — to Jerusalem and to the cross.

The Transfiguration

When Jesus questioned the disciples, asking them, *Who do you say that I am?*, it was Peter who confessed, *You are the Messiah, the Son of the Living God!* It is one of the few questions actually answered in our study. Grasping Peter's seed of belief, Jesus began to warn His disciples of what was to come.

> *From that time on Jesus began to explain to His disciples that He must go to Jerusalem and suffer many things at the hands of the elders, the chief priests and the teachers of the law, and that He must be killed and on the third day be raised to life.*[2]

They heard it I am sure, but it did not register. Have you ever been blindsided by a situation that sat right under your nose for a long period of time, and you missed it? It happened to me when my mother died. At my mother's funeral, a dear friend remarked how very pale and fragile my mother had looked six weeks earlier at my father's funeral. During those six weeks between both of my parents' funerals, I spent a week at home with my mother, and had two other visits with her. I never noticed what my friend saw - the thinning of her hair, dimming of her eyes, her grayish coloring, her overall weakness. I was blinded to it. As many times as Jesus told the disciples of His death and resurrection, they were blinded and deafened to what was right in front of them.

Soon after, Jesus took Peter, John, and James with Him to the top of a mountain to be alone and pray. These same three were at the bedside with Jairus and his young daughter. These same three would be singled out at Gethsemane to stay awake and pray. What they witnessed this day took months before they would understand, and years before they would write of it.

Jesus was transfigured. Before their eyes, His face changed and His clothes became dazzling white, brighter than the sun. I have always pictured this as if the earthly flesh of Jesus was unzipped, and from inside His body shone the full Glory of God. Scholars say the Transfiguration was a visible manifestation of God's presence in cloud and in light.[3] Jesus did not further reveal His identity in dialogue; this time the lesson was visual.

Peter, John, and James had been asleep. Yet, as they fully awoke, they saw with their own eyes Jesus in His glorified state. Before they could begin to absorb Who was before them, Moses and Elijah also appeared, speaking with Jesus. There is no conversation between the disciples; they are speechless. And they inherently recognized Moses and Elijah. The two prophets — Elijah taken up to God in a whirlwind, and Moses buried by God, are once again physically on the planet. Moses, as the Old Testament lawgiver, and Elijah, representing all the Old Testament prophets, are speaking with the Son of God.

Two men, Moses and Elijah, appeared in glorious splendor, talking with Jesus. They spoke about his departure, which he was about to bring to fulfillment at Jerusalem.[4]

Think on this

Moses and Elijah came to speak with Jesus about the cross.

The cross. A conversation so holy we know not a word of it. So glorious that words burst forth from Peter's lips, "Jesus, this is wonderful! Let's keep it this way forever. I will build three tabernacles and we will never leave this mountaintop!" *(my words)*. While Peter was speaking they were completely enveloped in a cloud, and from the cloud God spoke, *This is My beloved Son. I take delight in Him. Listen to Him!* The terrified disciples fell on their faces, and when they arose the cloud was lifted, Moses and Elijah gone. Jesus stood alone, the sole bearer of God's new revelation. Jesus told them not to tell anyone of the vision until after the Son of Man was raised from the dead.[5]

God allowed Peter, John, and James to see His splendor and hear His voice. God spoke the same words at Jesus' baptism and at the Transfiguration He added these words at the Transfiguration, *Listen to Him!* Thirty years later, this is what Peter had to say, encouraging the followers of Christ to pay close attention and believe in the truth of Scripture.

For we were not making up clever stories when we told you about the powerful coming of our Lord Jesus Christ. We saw his majestic splendor with our own eyes when he received honor and glory from God the Father. The voice from the majestic glory of God said to him, "This is my dearly loved Son, who brings me great joy." We ourselves heard that voice from heaven when we were with him on the holy mountain. Because of that experience, we have even greater confidence in the message proclaimed by the prophets. You must pay close attention to what they wrote, for their words are like a lamp shining in a dark place—until the Day dawns, and Christ the Morning Star shines in your hearts. Above all, you must realize that no prophecy in Scripture ever came from the prophet's own understanding, or from human initiative. No, those prophets were moved by the Holy Spirit, and they spoke from God.[6]

In almost every Bible study I have taught, there is one question that always surfaces, one question I have asked myself, many times. *How do we hear God?* God specifically says *to listen* to His Son, so how exactly do we do that? I feel slightly ridiculous answering such a weighty question. However, two points have helped me, and I hope will aid you in your desire to follow God more deeply.

Firstly, ***stay close to Scripture***. God speaks through His Word. All of it — New Testament and Old. I read the Bible to listen. Sometimes I learn something of God's character, sometimes I read to study a passage, sometimes I flip my Bible open randomly and read for sheer comfort. While I read, I listen for God's voice.

I have never heard God speak audibly; however, often the words roar off the page and I can go no further. Sometimes His is a gentle conviction, sometimes it is a nudge toward obedience, sometimes it is a simple gift of peace to my heart. I am never left stranded. He meets me there in His Word. Charles Spurgeon said it best, "Visit many good books but live in the Bible."[7] I read to listen.

Secondly, *do*. Do whatever he tells you. Mary said this to the servants at the wedding in Cana, and I personally believe spiritual growth is connected to obedience to God. When one intentionally listens to someone, listening is with the intention of doing. It is in this way that I listen to my daughters and daughters-in-law when they give instruction about our grandchildren. I intently listen in order to correctly do whatever they ask, for the safety of the children, and for the favor of their mothers.

The same with God. I read God's Word to listen, and I listen to do. I want to get it right for my well being, and for His favor. I certainly do not always get it right, not by a long shot. Yet, I fully believe that you and I can be much bolder in trusting that we do indeed hear Him, and then, in actually following and doing what it is He is telling us.

Think on this

God is not hiding all the clues and playing a game of hide and seek with His will.

God is not playing games with us. He loves us. If we are sincere, if we have prayed, if we know our decision does not negate Scripture's command, if we have His peace that passes human understanding, then we can more actively and passionately follow Jesus. If we get it wrong, and we will, the Holy Spirit will step in and check us. Many more times than I can count, I have hesitated, needing one more confirmation before making a decision. I have made wrong decisions thinking they were right, and right decisions, still second-guessing myself and God. I have met His grace and mercy, and

I have met His discipline. It is a part of our journey to *listen*, *learn*, and *do*, in order to *know* our great God. Jesus knows each of our hearts, and when we are sincere, He meets us where we are, and gives the next bit of light to our steps.

We are to the turn. We have a little further to go, carefully paying attention, before we can speed back up and head in a different direction with Jesus.

The Turn

After the Transfiguration and before the Feast of Tabernacles, there is one small significant section of Scripture that in my faith walk, I return to again and again. The change in Jesus is becoming more and more noticeable; by the Feast of Tabernacles it is marked and evident.

A man in the crowd answered, "Teacher, I brought you my son, who is possessed by a spirit that has robbed him of speech. Whenever it seizes him, it throws him to the ground. He foams at the mouth, gnashes his teeth and becomes rigid. I asked your disciples to drive out the spirit, but they could not."

"You unbelieving generation," Jesus replied, "how long shall I stay with you? How long shall I put up with you? Bring the boy to me." So they brought him. When the spirit saw Jesus, it immediately threw the boy into a convulsion. He fell to the ground and rolled around, foaming at the mouth. Jesus asked the boy's father, "How long has he been like this?" "From childhood," he answered. "It has often thrown him into fire or water to kill him. But if you can do anything, take pity on us and help us."

"'If you can'?" said Jesus. "Everything is possible for one who believes." Immediately the boy's father exclaimed, "I do believe; help me overcome my unbelief!" [8]

At the halfway point of our study, are you beginning to discern *the tone* of Jesus' voice? Can you detect the tenderness in His voice with the woman who touched His robe to be healed from her bleeding, His clarity with Jairus, His steady patience with the disciples, His authority with demons? In the above passage, do we hear His frustration? Jesus is incredulous when He says, *'If you can?' Everything is possible for the one who believes.*

Again, we return to *belief.* Here once more, Jesus uses the word *can.* Jesus is teaching belief, calling for belief, healing to prompt belief, doing miracles to point to belief. A ministry poured out so that we will believe. The father in this passage receives Jesus' rebuke, but turns on a dime. Immediately he says, *I do believe; help me overcome my unbelief!* Belief and unbelief in the same utterance.

In the Greek, the word "believe" in Mark 9:24, means "to commit, to trust, to entrust one's spiritual well being to Christ." The word "unbelief" translates "faithlessness, disobedience." [9] To myself, I paraphrase the father's reply to read something like this: "I do entrust my spiritual well being to Christ. Help my disobedience!" What honesty in the father's plea! Surely the desire for greater faith must have pleased Christ. Jesus cast the demon out of the boy, and the father's seed of belief was nourished and rewarded.

Jesus values honesty and He values belief. Even in answering His questions in this study, we can give a surface answer. I tried that at first; it was not satisfying. When I really answered the question as if Jesus was speaking to me in the same setting with the same words, I could not get away with a pat answer. I came back to my shallow answers again and again, like a dog to a bone — digging them up, gnawing and chewing on my answer. Until it was honest. When I am honest, I hear my own voices repeating the same words the father spoke. I want to say this to Christ almost every day of my life: "Lord, I trust you with the end result, I trust you with my salvation. But in the day to day life situations, emergencies, and trials, there are pockets of unbelief, doubt, and lack of trust in me. I do believe; help my unbelief!"

The Feast of Tabernacles

In the fall of the year, the Israelites celebrated the Feast of Tabernacles.

As the harvest ended and after the grapes, dates, figs, pomegranates and olives were gathered, all families congregated in Jerusalem for the most popular festival of the year. For seven days they celebrated *Sukkoth*, meaning *tabernacles*, and all Israel lived in booths, outdoor shelters made from branches, on rooftops, and lining the streets outside Jerusalem's city walls. It was like a great camp out with singing, parades, branch waving, and the familiar faith stories retold. On the eighth day, the feast culminated with the Great Day of Sukkoth. There is only one record of Jesus going to the Feast of Tabernacles. He went alone; it was a dangerous time for Him. It was the October before His death.

But when the Jewish Festival of Tabernacles was near, Jesus' brothers said to him, "Leave Galilee and go to Judea, so that your disciples there may see the works you do. No one who wants to become a public figure acts in secret. Since you are doing these things, show yourself to the world." For even his own brothers did not believe in him. Therefore Jesus told them, "My time is not yet here; for you any time will do. The world cannot hate you, but it hates me because I testify that its works are evil. You go to the festival. I am not going up to this festival, because my time has not yet fully come." After he had said this, he stayed in Galilee. However, after his brothers had left for the festival, he went also, not publicly, but in secret.[10]

Several days into the Feast of Tabernacles, Jesus arrived at the Feast and began to teach at the temple. The Jews doggedly challenged His authority, to which Jesus replied, *My teaching is not my own. It comes from the one who sent me. Anyone who chooses to do the will of God will find out whether my teaching comes from God or whether I speak on my own.* The Jews repeatedly inferred they believed this man to be a charlatan. Jesus said, *Yes, you know me, and you know where I am from. I am not here on my own authority, but he who sent me is true. You do not know him, but I know him because I am from him and he sent me.* The Jews arrogantly assumed they could seize and arrest Him at any time. Jesus said, *I am with you for only a short time, and then I am going to the one who sent me.*

Jesus' authority, origin, and destination all are questioned. Jesus boldly states His authority is given by God, His origin is from God, and He is returning to God. They tried to grab Him, wanted to kill Him, yet no one was able to lay a hand on Him. Jesus was a marked man, but not on their timetable, nor by their will.[11]

On the final day of Tabernacles, the Great Day of Sukkoth, two beautiful symbolic festivals brought the week to an end. At the Water Festival, priests drew water with a golden pitcher from the Gihon Spring, and made their way into Jerusalem through the Water Gate. Repeating the procession seven times, each time they climbed the steps to the altar, poured out the water until the altar was thoroughly soaked. Crowds followed singing and repeating psalms. The prayers were for the dry and thirsty land to be replenished at a time of drought, and bring abundance to the land and to the people. It was considered a blessing from God to have rainfall during Tabernacles. It was at the Water Festival that Jesus stood and spoke of Himself as the answer to their prayers, both physically and spiritually.

On the last and greatest day of the festival, Jesus stood and said in a loud voice, "Let anyone who is thirsty come to me and drink. Whoever believes in me, as Scripture has said, rivers of living water will flow from within them." By this he meant the Spirit, whom those who believed in him were later to receive.[12]

Held on the same day, The Light Festival was perhaps the most stunning event of the entire week. In the Temple's Court of the Women, four large stands held sixteen golden bowls brimming with oil. Knotted wicks were made from the priest's undergarments. Gary Burge writes, "When they were lit at night, all Jerusalem was illumined. In a world that did not have public lighting after dusk, this light shining from Jerusalem's yellow limestone walls must have been spectacular." [13] It is in this magnificent and momentous setting that Jesus said of Himself, *I am the light of the world. Whoever follows me will never walk in darkness, but will have the light of life.[14]*
By the time the Feast of Tabernacles drew to a close, Jesus, in multiple ways, had clearly revealed Himself. Tracing from His conversation with the Samaritan woman forward, the thread of His identity wove tangibly

through His ministry. Jesus met the people, cured their need, revealed Himself. At the feeding of the five thousand, He called Himself the Bread of Life. At the Water Festival, He pointed to Himself as the reliever of thirst, the Living Water. At the Light Festival, He revealed Himself as Light, the Light. Yet, continually, He was questioned. Everything about the identity of the Son of God was questioned. The discussion with the Jews became more heated, almost to the breaking point. Jesus turned to them and questioned their belief.

Pivotal Question #5

If I tell you the truth, why don't you believe me?

John 8:46

We are through the curve, traveling in quite a different direction, headed to the cross.

The work of God is this: to believe in the one he has sent.
- THE LORD JESUS CHRIST[15.]

I want to believe You. More than ever, I want to believe.
I want to please You. I don't know why I don't believe.
Because I am fearful. Because I can't make sense of it.
My pride gets in the way. Life gets in the way.
Identify to me the pockets of unbelief in my life and in my heart,
so that I can confess each one before You, and repent.
- EXCERPT FROM MY JOURNAL[16]-

Pivotal Question #5

If I tell you the truth, why don't you believe me?

John 8:46

Read the full passage *John 8:12-59.*

The Feast of Tabernacles is coming to a close and Jesus has turned a corner in His ministry. A permanent shift has taken place.

- Where is Jesus teaching and to whom?

Read the passage one more time.

- How has the subject matter changed?

- What words might lead us to believe Jesus' tone of voice has changed?

- Any additional thoughts?

- Was Jesus' question answered?

Ponder *John 8:42-47* before answering the pivotal question.

If Jesus asked you this question today, how would you respond to Him?

Why don't you and I believe Him?

Journal your answer. Pray over the question. Talk to Christ about your doubts, fears, and areas of unbelief. Take all the time you need, start and return to it, but get something down on paper.

The Man Born Blind

John 9:1-41

1. Where was Jesus, who was He with, and what day of the week was it?

2. What did Jesus do that He had never done before?

3. What was the question Jesus asked to the blind man?

4. Write out step by step how Jesus revealed Himself to the blind man *(verses 35-39)*.

5. Recount a time in your life when Jesus healed your spiritually blind eyes?

The Good Shepherd

John 10:1-21

This is a passage to camp out in for a little while. Read the passage and let it sit in your heart. It is easy to see why chapter 10 of John is a favorite. Following the rigidity, pettiness, and unbelief of the Pharisees in chapter 9, this chapter is a great comfort and strength to the believer.

6. How many times does Jesus say, *I tell you the truth*?

7. What are the truths Jesus puts forth?

8. List each time Jesus says *I AM* and reveals a new Name of Himself.

9. What was divisive for those with hard hearts became a lifeline to those who believed. What truth spoken by Jesus in this passage is the one you cling to above all others? Why?

The Last Public Ministry

Our lesson this week covers nine chapters of the Gospel of Luke, *Luke 10-18*. Jesus resolutely sets out for Jerusalem. No longer in Galilee, He attracts even larger crowds while teaching, healing, and driving out demons. He re-teaches certain lessons and begins to speak in parables again. In the face of dogged unbelief His language is strong and curt to the Pharisees, yet full of hope and life to his disciples and followers. It is almost as if we sense an urgency in His witness, and His burning desire to reach people before His time on earth comes to a end. He pulls His disciples close.

In Chapter 4, I mentioned ways to *Listen to Him* — God's words to Peter, John, and James at the Transfiguration. One of the ways to listen to Jesus is, after hearing His call, take action. **Do.** Jesus' mother, Mary, told the servants at the wedding in Cana, *do whatever He tells you.* Action. When we combine action with His call and our belief, the particular truth Jesus is teaching us personally is cemented in our hearts. This is the **do** part of our study this week.

Skim the parables in *Luke 12-18.* Choose **one parable** that will be yours for the next few weeks. Once you have decided on the specific parable, answer the following questions in preparation for doing.

10. The parable I chose *(title of parable and verses)* and why:

11. What is Jesus saying in this parable? Am I in the parable? What is Jesus saying to me?

12. Pray and ask God to show you a way to live out this particular parable in your life. It could be something as simple as sharing the lesson you have learned with a friend in need. You could write a letter, print a verse, pray Scripture back to God, make a phone call, write a poem or a song. In my case, I could possibly paint a parable. Pray and see what Jesus wants you to do. *Listen to Him.* Be creative, let your holy imagination take flight. *Do whatever He tells you.*

13. This may be a question to come back to in a few days, even weeks. But do come back. After you have prayed over your parable and lived it out in some way, you have actually taken Jesus at His word and responded with a unique obedience relevant to our day, our time. Record what you have learned about the heart of Jesus.

Learn to interpret
circumstances
by the love of
Christ and not
Christ's love by the
circumstances.

JAMES MONTGOMERY BOICE

CHAPTER 5

That You may Believe

The Lord will not always rescue you when you want Him to. And He certainly will not act according to your timetable every time. Sometimes He will let you die. In fact, He may wait until you're quadruply dead and stinking in your tomb before He does anything. So when things become black in your life, and there seems to be no way out, your situation has the fingerprints of Jesus Christ all over it. Chisel it in stone: you can't have a resurrection without a death. Resurrection is God's act alone. And that's why it always brings glory to Him.

- FRANK VIOLA[1]-

In John 10:22 we come to this phrase, *and it was winter*. It was winter on the calendar, the temperatures were low, the people wore thicker clothing, the land was cold and hard. Perceptive and introspective, John meant far more — it was winter in the cold, hard hearts of the Pharisees.

Think on this

Unbelief is cold, and if we have learned nothing else in these weeks, we know that it is belief and unbelief that Jesus was then, and is now, all about.

In hearts of stone, jealousy had turned to hatred. Three times the Pharisees had tried to kill Jesus.

> *Then came the Festival of Dedication at Jerusalem. It was winter, and Jesus was in the temple courts walking in Solomon's Colonnade. The Jews who were there gathered around him, saying, "How long will you keep us in suspense? If you are the Messiah, tell us plainly."*
>
> *Jesus answered, "I did tell you, but you do not believe. The works I do in my Father's name testify about me, but you do not believe because you are not my sheep. My sheep listen to my voice; I know them, and they follow me. I give them eternal life, and they shall never perish; no one will snatch them out of my hand. My Father, who has given them to me, is greater than all; no one can snatch them out of my Father's hand. I and the Father are one." Again the Jews picked up stones to stone him.*[2]

The door of ministry in Jerusalem was closing. The times were too perilous, the work was not finished. So Jesus left. *Then Jesus went back across the Jordan to the place where John had been baptizing in the early days. There he stayed... And in that place many believed in Jesus.*[3] He retreated to Perea, the area where John the Baptist's ministry ended and His ministry began. It was a place of blessing, a place where true belief took hold, the place where Jesus was baptized, the place He called His first disciples.

There is a lesson for us here. Have you ever felt as if God was backing you out from a place? Perhaps the timing was not right, and you felt you were not supposed to be there, live there, work there, go to church there, be engaged there, or be in ministry there? In confusion and frustration, you leave. Did Jesus retreat in defeat? No. James Boice in his commentary, *The Gospel of John*, writes, "Driven out of Jerusalem? Yes, in a sense. But not out of a place of God's blessing." [4]

Sometimes God's leading includes retreat.

I think we can all agree that Jesus' leading is not always going forward. Sometimes He says to wait, stop, stay; it may even include backing away. We may not have all the answers, only a sense of His leading. For years we may have questions. Sometimes our only option is to trust — trust in God's timing, trust that He is good, His plan is perfect and He is at work.

Jesus was continuing to teach, but God removed Him from the attack. He was being blessed by his Father. In the midst of the cold, there was a very warm place — the little village of Bethany.

The Place Jesus Loved

Bethany. Just two miles east of Jerusalem, it was a holy little village, a sacred space. Jesus was welcomed there, loved there. He visited there often, spent the nights of His last week on earth there; it was the last place his human feet touched earthly soil. And Jesus did his greatest miracle in Bethany.

Jesus' dear friends, a special family, lived in Bethany — older sister, Martha; younger sister, Mary; and their brother, Lazarus. I know this family, it is my birth family — Suzanne, Steph, and Rob. Even the personalities hold together. I am the older sister, planner and organizer; Steph is the middle child, the pensive, reflective one; Rob, the baby of the family upon whom everyone doted. I like to be reminded of what John wrote of the little family in Bethany, *Now Jesus loved Martha, her sister, and Lazarus*, and apply it to myself, "Now Jesus loves Suzanne, Steph, and Rob."

Lazarus became deathly ill and Jesus was notified. Knowing Jesus' affection for the family and the village, we are stunned He waited two full days before traveling to Lazarus' bedside. On purpose He delayed. He told his disciples, *Our friend Lazarus has fallen asleep; but I am going there to wake him up.* His disciples replied, *Lord, if he sleeps, he will get better.* Jesus had been speaking of his death, but his disciples thought he meant natural sleep. So then he told them plainly, *Lazarus is dead, and for your sake I am glad I was not there, so that you may believe. But let us go to him.*

I believe one of the hardest lessons we are forced to learn in life is when God says wait, when God delays in answering our request. The disciples did not understand Jesus' delay to go to Lazarus' side, nor did they understand why they were going back to a village all too near Jerusalem. Neither do we understand God's delays. Often we misinterpret the delay as Thomas did — that God cares little for our life or our concern.

We are wrong. God's delays are never out of indifference or that He is too busy or cares little.

 God uses delays to mold and strengthen our faith. James Boice gives us a valuable tool, *"Learn to interpret circumstances by the love of Christ and not Christ's love by the circumstances."*[7]

The Miracle Most Remembered

Jesus had a distinct and unique relationship with each member of the family. Too often we remember Martha as being the sister rebuked by Jesus when she complained about Mary not helping with the household duties. In this passage there is not a shadow of that rebuke hanging over her head. Martha was the first to go and meet Jesus when she heard He had arrived in Bethany. Their conversation is one of the most memorable in Scripture.

Martha relayed her grief to Jesus, saying if He had been in Bethany two days ago, she knew He could have saved her brother. Jesus replied to Martha, *Your brother will rise again.* Martha quickly affirmed her full belief, knowing that Lazarus would rise in the resurrection at the last day, referring to a later date in history. Did Jesus make light of her limited faith, her inability to understand His deeper meaning? No. He took her speck of faith and gently walked her to greater faith. Jesus said, *I am the resurrection and the life. The one who believes in me, even if he dies, will live. Everyone who lives and believes in me will never die — ever. Do you believe this?*[8]

In our times of deepest grief, we find comfort in these same words from Jesus. Do we believe this? Martha's faith at the time did not include a resurrection *the same day*. Jesus not only introduced her to a resurrection, He revealed Himself to her as *the resurrection*. I AM. Within the hour she would witness the resurrection of her brother; within days she would come to know the fruition of Jesus' words.

Mary heard that Jesus was calling for her. She ran to Him; she fell at His feet. Like Martha, Mary believed that if Jesus had arrived sooner there would have been hope for her brother. At this point, Jesus wept. He cried with and for his friends. John tells us that Jesus was *angry in his spirit and deeply moved*. His "sorrow was intermixed with anger at the evil of death, and also with a deep sense of awe at the power of God that was about to flow through him to triumph over death." [9]

Dr. Boice writes:

> "It is not an impassible, insensitive, unmovable Christ that is commended to you and me in Christianity. It is One who has entered into our grief and who understands our sorrow. Are you suffering? He knows it. Are you in tears? He has been there before you. Are you distressed? So was He. But he went on to overcome these things so that we might overcome them." [10]

Jesus was led to Lazarus' tomb with Martha and Mary and the many Jews who were in Bethany comforting the family. When Jesus commanded the tombstone be removed, Martha reminded Him that it had been four days; the body smelled. Jesus replied, *Didn't I tell you that if you believed you would see the glory of God?* He raised His voice to His Father saying, *I said this so they may believe you sent me.* **Believe.** Angry over death and unbelief, Jesus called Lazarus out of the tomb; He shouted with a loud voice, *Lazarus, come out!* [11] This miracle was to bring belief in the Son of God. And it did.

It is said that if Jesus had not called Lazarus by name, every tomb would have emptied its dead at His power. Dead four days, Lazarus, still wrapped in grave clothing, came out of the tomb. Back to life. Breathing, heart beating. Resurrected by The Resurrection.

The Question Most Often Asked

Jesus again retreated with his disciples to the countryside of Ephraim, continually teaching on the Kingdom of God. After Lazarus' resurrection, the threat of death was even more real. Wherever He turned, death lurked around every corner, waiting in the shadows. In time, He turned His sight to Jerusalem, knowing it would be His last trip, knowing what faced Him there.

Leaving Jericho, a blind man called out to Jesus for mercy. Jesus stopped and called Bartimaeus to Him, asking one question. Surprisingly, we have come to one question that is simply, boldly, and honestly answered.

I have a feeling Jesus asked this question often. We are told of several times in varying circumstances. Because it is quite different from "What are you looking for?", because it goes to our very core, we too will attempt to answer the question as Bartimaeus did — simply, boldly, and honestly.

Pivotal Question #6

What do you want me to do for you?

Matthew 20:32; Mark 10:36, 51; Luke 18:41

Unlocking Belief
Answering Questions Jesus Asks

What have I been trusting God would do? And today – the immediate present – is the third day, and He has not done it; therefore I imagine I am justified in being dejected and in blaming God. The meaning of prayer is that we get hold of God, not of the answer.
- OSWALD CHAMBERS[12]-

Ask for whatever you want me to give you.
- THE ALMIGHTY GOD[13]-

Pivotal Question #6

What do you want me to do for you?

Matthew 20:32; Mark 10:36, 51; Luke 18:41

With the emphasis on *for you*...

We come back to this question because Jesus came back to it. Several times. It is different from *What are you looking for?* or *What do you want?* Both of those questions were asked early in His ministry. Now, in two varying circumstances He asks, *What do you want me to do for you?*

In preparation to answering Jesus' question personally, read and note the answers in each of the following exchangs:

Matthew 20:17-22 & Mark 10:32-41
- To whom was Jesus speaking?
- What was Jesus asked to do?
- What was His reply?

Matthew 20:29-34; Mark 10:46-52; & Luke 18:35-43

- To whom was Jesus speaking?
- What was Jesus asked to do?
- What was His reply?

If Jesus asked you this question today, how would you respond to Him?

Answer each question as if you were alone with Jesus in your room, and He looked at you, eye to eye, and asked the question. Same words, same tone of voice. He is gentle and kind and loves you. There is no safer place to open your heart than to the heart of Christ.

Week 5 Study Guide

Just as Jesus' ministry has shifted and changed, our study does also. To the Pharisees, His questions have become more numerous, emphatic and pointed. To His disciples, his questions lessen in number, yet are more profound. We tread around His questions hesitantly, wishing not to answer, afraid not to.

Up to now we have been studying Jesus' travels, His teachings, exchanges with various people, his words, tone of voice, and the circumstances surrounding crucial points of his ministry. Now, we simply move into answering more of His questions and looking closely into the final private moments with His disciples. With every answer, I feel as if I draw nearer to His heart and more honest with my own.

Our study consists of two searing questions asked to the Pharisees and two heartfelt exchanges with the disciples. It is the last week of Jesus' life. He is staying in Bethany at night and traveling two miles into Jerusalem during the day to teach in the temple complex. A plot to kill Him is underway, however ironically, religious leaders are careful of the Passover timing, expecting riots if He were to be killed during the festival.

To the Pharisees:
Have you never read?

1. Read *Matthew 21:15-17; Matthew 21:42-46, Mark 12:9-12; Luke 20:17-19; Mark 12:24.* Jesus asked this question repeatedly. List several personal reasons why the Scriptures are meaningful or foundational in your life.

2. Read *Matthew 21:18-22*. Once again, Jesus places faith and doubt in the same sentence (verse 21). In light of all we have studied regarding Jesus' responses to belief and unbelief, what was the lesson Jesus had for His disciples?

3. What is the lesson Jesus has for you personally? Write out a simple prayer for a personal request you have today of Jesus.

To the Pharisees:
How can you escape being condemned to hell?

4. Read *Matthew 23:1-39*. In verses 33-39, what does Jesus say will keep a person from hell?

5. A believer has two answers to this question — a theological answer and a personal one. We take it very seriously. The theological answer points to the cross of Christ and the personal answer is our salvation story. ***How did you escape being condemned to hell?***

6. Where in God's Word do you find assurance and comfort that, as a believer in Christ, you have been rescued from hell?

The Disciples Asked:
What is the sign of your coming?

7. Spend some time reading *Matthew 24*. We may have read this passage previously, especially at times of world crisis or after 9/11. This time I am amazed how Jesus left nothing undone or untaught to those He loved.

Nothing needed was left out. He had not yet endured the cross, still He was preparing His own for His Second Coming. His warnings and His assurances were given to them; they belong to us also. What truths about His Second Coming stand out to you today?

8. Just past the halfway point in our study seems like a good time to return, reread and review our answers to the previous six questions. If you have additional insights, add them. Be sure to leave empty pages in your journal after each question, so that as you reflect upon them again and again, even answering them at a different time in your life, you will have lots of white space for the many truths God is desiring to give.

If we desire to know the heart of Jesus Christ, it is revealed on this night, in the Passover, with His dearest friends, as He takes the role of the sacrificial Lamb of God. Sacrifice, servanthood, love — to lead us to belief. ⦵⊢≡

CHAPTER 6

Private Moments

Search all my sense, and know my heart,
Who only canst make known,
And let the deep, the hidden part
To me be fully shown.

Search, till thy fiery glance has cast
Its holy light through all,
and I by grace am brought at last
Before thy face to fall.

Thus prostrate I shall learn of thee,
What now I feebly prove,
That God alone in Christ can be
Unutterable love.

- FRANCIS BOTTOME[1]-

There has never been a Passover like this one — before or since. We are not surprised that Jesus was in Bethany the week before Passover. It was there He spent the last nights of His earthly life. He traveled to Jerusalem the early part of the week and returned to Bethany every night. He taught during the day, yet when away from the crowds, Jesus poured His heart into His disciples and close friends. Although they did not yet realize it, these intense and intimate private moments with the Son of God were to be the backbone of faith for the first believers and the beginnings of the church.

A banquet was held at the home of Simon the Leper, and only Mary of Bethany innately understood Jesus' future days. Perhaps she had been listening when all the disciples were arguing. What happened at the banquet is recorded by Matthew, Mark, and John and is remembered to this day. Mary came in to a room full of men, knelt down at Jesus' feet as He was reclining at table, and let down her hair. She then broke open a costly jar of pure nard, perfumed oil imported from India, and poured it over His feet, wiping His feet with her long hair. The disciples were shocked, offended, and talk began amongst them. Jesus, gave no sense of impropriety to Mary's actions. He commended her. *Why are you bothering this woman? She has done a noble thing for me. You always have the poor with you... you do not always have me. She has anointed my body in advance for burial.*[2]

Mary's reputation could have been ruined by her actions; instead, she was validated by Jesus. It took great faith and love to do what she did. Mary's gift was costly, worth a year's salary. There are very few things we purchase in life worth a year's salary. Some believe that she could have been saving her perfume for her future marriage, her dowry. Giving it to Jesus was a great sacrifice. The amount of oil was equivalent to half a liter by today's standard. The air must have been heavy with the aroma. There was no mistaking what Mary had done. She did not sneak in to quietly honor Jesus; her act was public. The fragrance alone filled everyone in the room with her remarkable gift. The scent would have lasted, saturating deep into Jesus' pores. Her gift was abundant, extravagant.

Think on this

Sacrifice for Jesus is honored by Jesus.

Jesus instructed the disciples to begin preparations for their Passover meal. The days prior were abuzz with activity. The room where they would celebrate Passover had been determined. Some of the disciples had to clean the room completely from any remnant of dust and yeast. A few went to purchase the lamb, the most perfect one they could find. The day before Passover from four to six in the afternoon, the lambs were brought to the temple stations which spread throughout the temple area. Over five thousand lambs were in the city, coupled with 100,000 visitors. Hundreds of Levites were on duty for the sacrifices. At three loud shofar blasts the lambs were killed, their blood drained, their blood poured on the altar, the carcass cleaned and given back to the family to roast. Gary Burge writes, "The entire scene must have been remarkable. The city was filled with the noise of the lambs, their cry at slaughter, the loud singing of large male choirs, the echo of shofar blasts, and the smell of roasted meat from every corner of the city. To do this each year for your life left indelible memories unifying Israel to its great story of Moses and the Exodus." [3]

On the day of Passover, with all preparations completed, the disciples met with Jesus. He said, *I have fervently desired to eat this Passover with you before I suffer. For I tell you, I will not eat it again until it is fulfilled in the Kingdom of God.* [4] Jesus had been looking forward to this time, this Passover — alone with His disciples, partaking in the holy tradition, celebrating the service commanded by God to commemorate the Exodus. He was anticipating the fellowship, preparing to break all boundaries and wash their feet, instituting a new covenant, becoming the sacrificial lamb. Jesus *desired* this. Fervently desired.

The Kiddush

The Passover service was organized by four cups of red wine taken during the dinner. At the first cup, the Kiddush, the Cup of Holiness, all the disciples stood and Jesus gave thanks, asking that the day be set apart to God. They then read the first half of the Hallel, Psalms 113-118. It was after the first cup that Jesus washed the disciples' feet. [5] That Jesus would take on the role of a servant, stoop with towel in hand and touch their feet, was shocking, offensive, humiliating. My church hosts a foot washing service during Holy Week, as part of the Maundy Thursday service. I have listened (and agreed) to reasons men and women do not want to participate — it is embarrassing, feet smell, feet are disfigured, nobody touches my feet. I have participated and washed someone's feet with no qualms. But, *my* feet? I had to swallow my pride to allow another person, even my husband, to kneel before me and take my feet in their hands. It is indeed humbling.

Peter was the disciple to voice his offense. Jesus carefully explained that in order to become one of His own, they must be washed clean. Jesus gently mentioned to Peter that he would understand later. When Jesus reclined back at the table, He asked the first question of three that we will answer this week: *Do you know what I have done for you?*[6]

Servanthood for Jesus is honored by Jesus.

At this point, we must remind ourselves that the disciples had no idea what was to come in the next hours. They were simply celebrating Passover and halfway expecting some kind of coup when Jesus would reveal Himself to the Roman government officials and become King. Or some version of that. Never would they have imagined that a foot washing began the countdown to Jesus finally and fully revealing His love, sacrifice, and servanthood. John, the disciple, summed it up by writing, *He loved them to the end.*[7]

The Maggrid

The second cup, the Maggrid, began the retelling of the Passover story. As each of the ten plagues were remembered, a tiny bit of wine was poured and drunk. The meal was enjoyed as each part of the Exodus story was retold and explained. The bitter herbs represented the years of slavery in Egypt; the lamb shank represented the lamb's blood put on the doorframe to show the family's belief in the One True God and allowed that family to be "passed over" from destruction. Each person would eat a piece of unleavened bread, the matzah, dipped in horseradish, then in a sweet apple mixture. The dipping of the matzah was a reminder of the sweetness of God's redemption in the midst of their bitter slavery.[8] It was at the dipping of the matzah that John asked Jesus who would be his betrayer. Jesus replied, *"He's the one I give the piece of bread to after I have dipped it." When he had dipped the bread, he gave it to Judas, Simon Iscariot's son. After Judas ate the piece of bread, Satan entered him. Therefore Jesus told him, "What you're doing, do quickly."*[9]

Judas, after taking the matzah, left the Passover feast. John inserts one sentence, *And it was night.*[10] Yes, the night was dark, the sky black, but John is revealing a darkness that settled on Jesus, on everyone present, on the world and on mankind. It was the time of the fullness of evil. Jesus knew His betrayal was in the works, He knew His hours were limited with the other eleven disciples. He knew.

It is now that the truly private, intimate moments with Jesus began. He said to them, *I give you a new command: love one another. Just as I have loved you, you must also love one another. By this all people will know that you are my disciples, if you have love for one another.*[11]

It was in this conversation that Jesus knowingly told the disciples He was headed to death. Peter boldly voiced he would follow Jesus to death, and all the disciples claimed the same allegiance. Jesus told them they would all scatter, and that Peter would deny him, indeed before the rooster crowed the next morning. In a dialog mentioned only by Luke, we find the second of three questions we will answer. Jesus reminded the disciples how they were cared for when He earlier sent them out to teach and heal. He said, *Did you lack anything?*[12]

The Birkat Hamazon

At this point in the Passover service Jesus picked up the third cup of wine, the Birkat Hamazon, the Cup of Redemption, celebrating Israel's blessings from God. It is believed this is when Christ broke tradition and instituted the Lord's Supper.[13] The disciples must have been astounded as Jesus broke bread saying, *This is my body, which is given for you. Do this in remembrance of Me.* He shared the cup saying, *This cup is the new covenant established by My blood; it is shed for you.*[14] The disciples partook, following Jesus' lead; it is not recorded if they spoke a word.

After the third cup, Jesus said to his disciples, *Your heart must not be troubled. Believe in God; believe also in me.* In eleven verses, Jesus mentions belief six times. When Philip asks to be shown the Father in order to believe, Jesus asked the third question we will answer: *Have I been with you so long and you still do not know me?* [15]

And here we are, back to belief. If we desire to know the heart of Jesus Christ, it is revealed on this night, in the Passover, with His dearest friends, as He takes the role of the sacrificial Lamb of God. Sacrifice, servanthood, love — to lead us to belief. Believe. Is there any doubt what He wants us to do?

Think on this

Belief in Jesus is honored by Jesus.

The Hallel

Jesus continued with the most beautiful words, words that have sustained believers over the centuries. Words of love, peace, promises of the Holy Spirit. Jesus prayed for the ones who would believe in Him. [16] The disciples and Jesus all sang, the Passover came to a close, and the little party moved out from the upper room into the night, headed to the familiar Garden of Gethsemane.

But wait. The fourth cup, the Hallel, the Cup of Praise, was it omitted? There is no mention of it in Scripture, leading some scholars to conclude that Jesus left off the fourth cup for His eternal purpose. Gary Burge writes, "Did Jesus never complete the meal? Did he not permit the drinking of the final cup? And if this was intentional, it means that Jesus left His followers (ourselves included) in a suspended Passover liturgy that can only be completed when we join Christ in heaven." [17]

After studying Passover and the missing fourth cup in Scripture, I have begun to believe that Jesus intentionally left off the fourth cup, and this is the cup Jesus meant when He said, *For I tell you, from now on I will not drink of the fruit of the vine until the kingdom of God comes.*[18] At a future date, Jesus will gather His own and share the fourth cup. Until then, when I take communion I often remember that it is the fourth cup to look forward to, sharing the Cup of Praise face to face with the One worthy of all praise.

The night of nights continued, yet before we move on we have three questions to answer.

Pivotal Question #7

Do you know what I have done for you?

John 13:12

Pivotal Question #8

Did you lack anything?

Luke 22:35

Pivotal Question #9

Have I been with you so long and still you do not know me?

John 14:9

But I also enjoy the idea that Jesus in some manner interrupted his final Passover meal. If he ended the meal abruptly and never completed the four-cup sequence of the Jewish liturgy ("I will not drink again from the fruit of the vine until that day when I drink it new in the kingdom of God." Mark 14:25), he has left each of us within the church living in a suspended Passover season. In this sense, the church lives within Passover, continually celebrating the meal that lives at the center of its worship and anticipating the moment when we join Christ in heaven and drink the final cup – the cup of praise and rejoicing, the Hallel cup – with him.

-GARY BURGE [19]-

No. I lack nothing that is needed: food, shelter, health, love. You have given me abundance. When You have sent me out I've had everything I needed. To teach, retreats, to write, to paint, to serve, to give, to listen, to mentor. You have even given me the very words, thoughts that I needed. Expertise, resources — a deep well that has refreshed itself over and over. When it comes to my heart, my relationship with You, with Your Father — I am lacking. Something holds me back. My faith, my trust, my belief — they waver at times. My humility is false. My resolve is judgmental. My love is little. I am coming to a place where I deeply desire and want to ask — for a stronger faith.

- AN EXCERPT FROM MY JOURNAL.[20]-

Do you know what I have done for you?

John 13:12

Did you lack anything?

Luke 22:35

Have I been with you so long and still you do not know me?

John 14:9

Jesus asks each of these three questions to His disciples during the Passover feast before His death on the cross. Time is running short. There are no more months or days in Jesus' ministry, only hours. Read the back story in *John 13:1-20, Luke 22:35-38,* and *John 14:1-14.*

If Jesus asked you these questions today, how would you respond to Him?

Have you found that your answers are becoming more and more honest? Do you feel the layers of your resistance peeling away? Are you letting your underbelly show to Jesus, are you drawing closer to Him? For me, yes, yes, and yes. The freedom of getting to the honest place! We can be completely honest with the Lord Jesus because He is our safe person.

Week 6 Study Guide

There is no additional study this week due to the gravity of answering the three questions posed to the disciples at Passover, and of what is to come.

Of the hundreds of questions Jesus asked during His lifetime, we are now down to less than thirty. The last two sessions of our study will take a bird's eye view of the remaining questions.

Our next chapter, Chapter 7, *The Way of the Cross*, is a careful study of the week leading to Jesus' crucifixion and a somber look at the cross. We are on Most Holy Ground.

The world went dark. Completely dark. It was a supernatural darkness we know nothing of, so deep, so profound that no person could view God's Son as He carried sin, as He bore man's sin in His body. ○——⚷

The Way of the Cross

God made him who had no sin to be sin for us,
so that in him we might become the righteousness of God.
- PAUL, A SERVANT OF CHRIST JESUS[1]-

On the holiest of ground, we are headed with Jesus to the cross. After leaving the Passover supper, Jesus relayed vital words of life to His disciples on the way to the Garden of Gethsemane. *I still have many things to tell you, but you can't bear them now. When the Spirit of truth comes, He will guide you into all the truth.*[2] Jesus' human conversations were coming to an end and everything else to be understood would be later, much of it falling to the able and trustworthy role of the Holy Spirit.

Jesus and his band of disciples arrived at the Garden, a place Jesus had visited often. He liked to pray there. Deep into the Garden He took Peter, John and James, while He went further to pray. Three times He returned to them, three times He implored them to stay awake, pray — pray that they not enter into temptation. Jesus finally asked, *Couldn't you stay awake with me one hour? Why are you sleeping?*[3] How many times have I felt the weight of that question when desperately needing to pray, but caving in to sleep. Why couldn't I stay awake even one hour? The disciples did not know what to say to Him and they could not keep their eyes open. Luke says they were exhausted from their grief.[4]

While Jesus was praying, while the three disciples were sleeping, the final decision of the cross was made. His resolution, decision, and unswerving commitment was made at Gethsemane.

Three times, Jesus prayed and asked the Father if there was any way possible to be spared from drinking the cup. Each time, Jesus ended His prayer saying, nevertheless, *not my will, but yours, be done.*[5] Two cups are mentioned in Scripture — one is the cup of salvation, and here, Jesus was referring to the second cup, the cup of God's wrath. The cup of God's wrath is the cup of righteous judgment to be poured out on man's sin. Luke tells us Jesus was in great anguish, so much so that His sweat became drops of blood.[6] Physicians today say this is indeed possible. Under great and extreme duress, human capillaries can rupture, causing blood to mix with sweat and seep through the pores. An angel came and strengthened Jesus, and the third time He arose from prayer, Jesus was resolute. His time had come.

The Betrayal

Judas knew the place, Gethsemane; he had often been with Jesus there. He led a large, armed band of soldiers, temple police, Pharisees and priests. During His arrest, Jesus asked four questions, each one of great importance. The first is when Jesus approached and inquired of the mob, *Who is it you are looking for?* When they replied, *Jesus the Nazarene,* Jesus simply responded, *"I am He." When he spoke the words I am He, they stepped back and fell to the ground.*[7] If this were not the unfounded arrest of the Son of God and of utmost seriousness, it could almost be comical. An armed band, military men, falling down and all over themselves at Jesus' words. The Great I AM replies, *I am.* James Boice has this to say, "It may well have been that he used his own great name, Jehovah, the name above every name, and that hearing this name uttered by the God-man threw the arresting party into

utter confusion and rendered them helpless even to stand before him." 8
Jesus must have waited for them to regain their footing before asking again,
Who is it you're looking for?

Judas, are you betraying the Son of Man with a kiss? 9 Jesus asked Judas one
question — the question that would be Judas' ultimate demise. At this
point the entire evening could have dissolved into chaos. The mob was
angry, the disciples were caught off guard, Judas' actions were confusing.
The evil one was at work. The moment men from the mob took hold of
Jesus to arrest him, Peter drew his sword and sliced off the ear of the high
priest's slave. The disciples could have been killed, Jesus could have been
killed, and the cross could have been thwarted, had Jesus not quickly,
calmly, touched the slave's ear, completely and immediately healing him.
Jesus turned to Peter, and proving His decision was made, asked, *Am I not
to drink the cup the Father has given me?* Jesus turned and asked the crowd, *Have
you come out with swords and clubs, as though I were a criminal to capture me?* 10 Jesus
was then arrested and every disciple fled.

The Trials

Books have been written on Jesus' trials. There were six trials, all held in
the middle of the night and earliest morning hours. The first three were
Jewish; the last three, Roman. In our study we will briefly touch on each
trial, noting Jesus' questions, or lack thereof. Ask the Holy Spirit to give
you insight as you note to whom Jesus asks a question and to whom He is
silent. We will skim through the trials; our true goal is the cross.

Jesus is first taken to Annas, the former High Priest, but the one who still
held the power. Caiaphas, the reigning High Priest, was married to Annas'
daughter. Annas questioned Jesus about His teachings and Jesus answered
with two questions, *I haven't spoken anything in secret. Why do you question me?*
Jesus was slapped by the temple police for being disrespectful. Then Jesus
asked, *If I have spoke wrongly, give evidence about the wrong; but if rightly, why do
you hit me?* 11 Two questions were asked, both revealing that it was Jesus'
intent to bring forth a specific charge for His arrest. In both Jewish and
Roman law, there had to be a charge.

Jesus was taken from Annas' residence in the temple complex to Caiaphas, the acting High Priest. Present were the chief priests, elders, and scribes. Looking for evidence against Jesus, many false witnesses were brought forth. After their testimonies, Caiaphas stood up and asked Jesus, *Don't you have an answer?* Jesus was silent. Again Caiaphas questioned, *Are you the Messiah?* Jesus answered, *I am, and all of you will see the Son of Man seated at the right hand of the Power and coming with the clouds of heaven.* At that Caiaphas tore his robes and claimed blasphemy. Jesus was spit upon, blindfolded, beaten and slapped.[12]

Meanwhile Peter was following at a distance. This one line is repeated in all four Gospels and all four interject this pivotal interlude — Peter's denial of Christ. The words, *following at a distance*, convey Peter's continued overconfidence and impulsiveness, his failure to pray as Jesus had earlier commanded, and resulted in Peter *standing with others*, rather than with Jesus. Three times, Peter declared he did not know Jesus. Once to a servant girl in the courtyard, again by the fire, and finally an hour later with insistence, cursing, and swearing an oath, *I do not know the Man!*[13]

Immediately, while he was still speaking, a rooster crowed. Then the Lord turned and looked at Peter. And he went outside and wept bitterly.[14] Jesus *looked at* Peter. Jesus was being led through the temple courtyard from Caiaphas' residence to the council of the Sanhedrin at the exact moment of Peter's third denial. While swearing, Peter must have gazed across the courtyard when his eyes met and locked with Jesus' eyes. In the Greek, the word "looked" means "looking all the way through someone or looking with knowledge of the person."[15] As Peter remembered Jesus' words predicting his denial, he ran from the courtyard and bitterly wept. It was *the look* that broke Peter.

Of all the things true of Peter (impulsiveness, overconfidence), Peter deeply loved Jesus, tried to defend Jesus, and was the first to confess Jesus as the Son of God. William Barclay is quick to point out that Peter was no coward. "The tremendous thing about Peter was that his failure was a failure that could only have happened to a man of superlative courage."[16] This was the fall of a big man, a big failure, a big shame. With it brought a big repentance and a big witness.

At daylight, Jesus was brought before the Sanhedrin. Still attempting to confirm a charge against Jesus, they demanded, *If you are the Messiah, tell us.*

Jesus responded, *If I do tell you, you will not believe. And if I ask you, you will not answer.* They asked, *Are you then, the Son of God?* and Jesus answered, *You say that I am.*[17] No questions from Jesus; the time for questions is running out.

With their false evidence of the charge of blasphemy, the Sanhedrin took Jesus to Pilate, the Roman governor. Pilate, attempting again to clarify the charge, asked Jesus one question, *Are you the King of the Jews?* Jesus answered with the one question he asked of Pilate, a question that forced Pilate to own his words and actions, *Are you asking this on your own, or have others told you about me?* Pilate continued his barrage of questions and Jesus inserted one brief statement of His kingdom, concluding with, *I have come into the world for this: to testify to the truth. Everyone who is of the truth listens to my voice.* Pilate flippantly replied, *What is truth?*[18] From that point Jesus answered no charge.

Jesus came to the world to testify to the Truth. To Himself. The One Who is Truth was charged with a lie.

Pilate sent Jesus to his enemy, Herod Antipas, who was in Jerusalem at the time. Herod Antipas was the Herod who had John the Baptist beheaded and was the grandson of Herod the Great, who issued the edict for the death of infant boys at the time of Jesus' birth. Herod Antipas was delighted to see Jesus, in fact, Herod and Pilate became friends that very day. Herod was hoping to question the celebrity teacher, maybe witness some never-before-seen miracles. Jesus said nothing; He was completely silent.

Having been mocked by Herod and his soldiers, Jesus, donned in a brilliant robe, is sent back to Pilate. Pilate told the priests and leaders that he had found no charge against Jesus, nor had Herod. Pilate planned to have Jesus whipped and released, but the priests cried for the murderer, Barabbas, to be released instead. Pilate had Jesus flogged. A crown of thorns was crushed into His head. Pilate paraded Jesus to the crowd, announced his famous words, *Here is the man!* To loud shouts of *crucify him, crucify him,* Pilate retreated inside for one last conversation with Jesus. Pilate repeated, *Where are you from?* Jesus was silent. Pilate again, *Don't you know I have the authority to release you and the authority to crucify you?* **Jesus spoke to Pilate,** *You would have no authority over me at all if it hadn't been given you from above.* **From the audience the cries grew louder and the arguments stronger. Pilate succumbed and handed Jesus over to be crucified.**[19]

The Cross

In this study, we have read through tens of questions Jesus asked; we have studied and answered nine. Can we fathom that Jesus, in his earthly body, has only two more questions to ask of mankind?

The cross was within view. Jesus was barely able to walk, battered beyond recognition. On the way to Golgotha, with Simon of Cyrene carrying His cross, Jesus turned to the multitude of people following Him and spoke to the women, *Daughters of Jerusalem, do not weep for me, but weep for yourselves and your children... For if they do these things when the wood is green, what will happen when it is dry?* The *English Standard Version Study Bible* notes, "For if they do these things when God's son is innocent, how much more will God's wrath be upon a sinful nation?" [20] This warning most likely speaks of the siege of Jerusalem and destruction of the temple in 70 A.D. I believe the meaning is broader than that one event. If the Son of God, the Son of Man, in the fullness of the Holy Spirit was crucified, what disasters will we encounter when His Spirit is one day removed from our world?

Much has been recorded of the last statements of Jesus' life. As He was crucified, He asked of God, *Father, forgive them for they do not know what they are doing.* During the first three hours of unfathomable agony on the cross, Jesus saved the believing criminal crucified next to Him as He said, *I assure you: today you will be with me in paradise.* And in compassion He looked down from the cross and spoke to His mother and to John, *Woman, here is your son* and *Here is your mother.*[21]

 The cross then became silent. Darkness covered the land for the next three hours, from noon until three o'clock. The world went dark. Completely dark. It was a supernatural darkness we know nothing of, so deep, so profound that no person could view God's Son as He carried sin, as He bore man's sin in His body, as Jesus drank the cup of God's wrath. We know from God's Word that Jesus became sin. *Became sin.*

God made Him who had no sin to be sin for us, so that in Him we might become the righteousness of God. II Cor 5:21

Think on this

Jesus becoming sin was the work of the cross.

During that darkness, Jesus asked the one question while on the cross, His one recorded question asked of God, His last question while on earth. *Eloi, Eloi, lema sabachthani? My God, My God, why have you forsaken me?[22]*

Jesus asked this question of God because God utterly and completely deserted Jesus while He was on the cross. While He was sin and while He drank the full cup of God's wrath. In our hardest days, we can *feel* God has deserted us. However, in truth, He has not. God has given us His Son. God has given believers His Spirit. Further, we have His promise that He will never leave us.

We answer this question because Jesus can ask it of us. If we are honest, we know that we have deserted Him many times in many ways.

Pivotal Question #10

Why have you forsaken me?

Matthew 27:46; Mark 15:34

The first verse (Psalm 22:1) speaks of Christ having been forsaken. I have read good books suggesting that Jesus was not really forsaken by God, that he only imagined he was forsaken, that Jesus almost lost his faith in God but he recovered it later when he knew that God had sustained him. This is wrong. Christ was bearing the penalty for sin, which is death, and death means separation from God. What is death? Certainly not physical death alone, but spiritual death! And spiritual death is the separation of the soul from the source of life, which is God. That is the penalty Christ bore for human sin — separation from God. So when he cried out in a loud voice, "My God, my God, why have you forsaken me?" it was the cry of one actually abandoned by the Father.

-JAMES MONTGOMERY BOICE[23]-

Pivotal Question #10

Why have you forsaken me?

Matthew 27:46; Mark 15:34

Read *Psalm 22*.

Right in the middle of the seven statements of Christ from the cross, comes *the one question* He asked of God, *My God, my God, why have you forsaken me?*

The word "forsaken" means, in the Greek, "to leave behind in some place, to desert."

In dire circumstances, in our our human-ness, in our frailty and pain, we wonder and sometimes cry out to God, asking why we have been left out, left behind or deserted. Jesus asked this question to God. He asked it for Himself; He asked it for us. Jesus was utterly forsaken so that, in Him, we will never be. His promise to us stands as a pillar of truth, *And surely I am with you always, to the very end of the age.*[24]

Jesus can, however, ask this question to us. It may be easier for us to answer *how* we have forsaken Him, or *when* we deserted Him; yet He lovingly asks us, *Why?*

What is your response to our Savior, our Friend?

If Jesus asked you this question today, how would you respond to Him?

Week 7 Study Guide

Our entire study this week is to create a timeline: 40 questions that take us from the Cross through the Resurrection, tracking the final questions of the risen Jesus. It is simple to do. It is like an open book quiz, most of the answers come straight from Scripture. The time it takes is well worth it — once completed, you will have a valuable reference tool for a lifetime.

I have found that I pull out this particular study guide every Lenten season. One friend suggested answering one question a day through the 40 days of Lent. Preparing for Easter, I like having these facts from Scripture at my fingertips. The effort taken now, to answer 40 questions, will pay rich dividends in years to come.

1. *Matthew 27:51 –52* mentions three things that happened suddenly after Jesus' death. They were:

        1.

        2.

        3.

2. In *Matthew 27:55-56,* the women observing the cross from a distance were:

        1.

        2.

        3.

3. In *Mark 15:42-46* and *John 19:39-40,* one man asked Pilate for Jesus' body and one man offered myrrh and aloe for burial. Who were they?

        1.

        2.

4. Several things happened the next day in *Matthew 27:62-66*. What were they?

5. From *Matthew 28:1-8* and *Mark 16:1-8*, list in sequence what happened shortly after sunrise on the first day of the week:

6. Who went to the tomb first?

7. Upon reaching the tomb, what were they planning to do?

8. What happened before they reached the tomb?

9. Who spoke to them at the tomb?

10. What five things did the angel tell the women?

        1.
        2.
        3.
        4.
        5.

11. In *Mark 16:7*, what phrase is added to the angel's words?

12. Why do you think this is significant? Remember, it is believed that Peter probably dictated his gospel to Mark.

13. With what emotion did they depart the tomb?

14. Where did they go?

15. From *Luke 24:9-12* and *John 20:2-10*, which two disciples left for the
    tomb after hearing the testimony of the women?

> 1.
> 2.

16. Which disciple reached the tomb first?

17. What caused John to believe?

18. From *John 20:11-18*, which woman stayed at the tomb?

19. What was she doing?

20. What two questions did Jesus ask her? These questions were the
    first He asked after His resurrection.

> 1.
> 2.

21. Who did she suppose the man speaking to her to be?

22. What was it that made her know it was Jesus?

23. What did Mary announce to the disciples?

24. From *Matthew 28:9-10*, who did Jesus appear to after first appearing to
    Mary Magdalene?

25. Where were the disciples to go?

26. From *Matthew 28:11-15*, what story was circulated to the public?

27. From *Luke 24:13-32*, to whom did Jesus appear next?

28. What was the topic of conversation?

29. From *Luke 24:26*, what question did Jesus ask the two?

30. From *Luke 24:30-32*, what opened their eyes?

31. What words did they use to describe their emotions as they were listening to Jesus explain the Scriptures?

32. From *Luke 24:36-37* and *John 20:19*, who did Jesus appear to next and what day was it?

33. From *Luke 24:38*, what two questions did Jesus ask?

34. In *Luke 24:39-43*, what were the three ways Jesus dispelled their doubts?
    1.
    2.
    3.

35. Who was not with them at the time?

36. From *John 20:26-31*, how many days was it before Jesus appeared a second time to the disciples?

37. What were Jesus' words to Thomas?

38. From *John 21:1-14*, where did Jesus appear to the disciples a third time?

39. In *John 21:7*, who was the disciple to recognize Jesus first?

40. In *John 21:7*, what was the response of Peter?

Jesus' questions are needed to pry away the masks we all wear. They are to bring us to honesty. And vulnerability, praying prayers we never have prayed before, having courage to ask for things and admit things we never have before.

CHAPTER 8

The Question of All Time

The Lord does three things. First He asks a question. The point of the question is to reveal to the disciples their own need and failure. God did not ask these questions because he did not know the answers. God asks questions to get us to face the situation. This leads to the next step in the story, for after having asked his question the Lord next gives a command. The point is not where the work is to be done or how. It is whether it is being done under Christ's direction and in obedience to him or by our own wisdom and initiative. Third, the Lord sends blessings. Now in response to their obedience to his command, Jesus sends such a great catch of fish that they are unable to draw the catch to land. But when they obeyed his instructions and so participated in the blessing of the great catch of fish, they made the discovery that this was the Lord.
-JAMES MONTGOMERY BOICE [1]-

While on the cross, Jesus, as the human Son of Man, asked His last question. Is He through asking questions? No. Not at all.

After the resurrection at the tomb, the Risen Christ asked Mary Magdalene, *Woman, why are you crying? Who is it you are looking for?* To the disciples walking to Emmaus, Jesus asked, *Didn't the Messiah have to suffer these things and enter into his glory?* And that evening when He appeared to the disciples He said, *Why are you troubled?* [2]

The disciples had been told to go to Galilee and wait for Jesus. While waiting, Peter decided to go fishing. After an all-nighter with no catch, the fishermen hear a man from the shore calling, *You don't have any fish, do you?* [3] They knew it was Jesus when they cast their nets as He instructed and the nets became too heavy to carry from the weight of fish.

Picture this. On a beach in early morning. The warmth and aroma of a charcoal fire. Breakfast. A victorious catch of 153 fish. Jesus with them again. Sitting around the campfire Jesus singled out Peter, asking, *Simon, son of John, do you love me more than these?* [4] Jesus uses Peter's old name, Simon. Jesus asks the question in front of everyone.

For the sake of deeper understanding let's read the exchange between Jesus and Peter with the Greek translations of the word "love."

> **Jesus:** *Do you love me with* **agape love** *— fully, unconditionally, completely, more than these other disciples?*

> **Peter:** *You know that I love you like a brother, with* **phileo love**.

> **Jesus:** *Do you love me with* **agape love** *— fully unconditionally, completely?* Jesus mercifully drops the comparison.

> **Peter:** *You know that I love you like a brother, with* **phileo love**.

> **Jesus:** *Do you love me with* **phileo love**, *like a brother?* Jesus speaks at Peter's level.

> **Peter:** *Lord, you know everything. You know I love you* **phileo**, *like a brother.* [5]

After Jesus repeated the question to Peter three times, the Bible says Peter was "grieved." The word "grieved" means "to make sorry, to be in heaviness." [6] This is a greatly subdued Peter, the beginning of a changed man. Peter is not saying he does not love Christ; he does, deeply. What he is not doing is boasting of his love, and above all, he is not saying it is more than someone else's love. He admits in front of everyone and to his Lord that his love is lacking. He is vulnerable, honest, and sincere.

It is the pointed, three-fold repetition that is painful to Peter, yet Dr. Boice has this to say about the exchange, "Yet in the ultimate analysis it was not cruel. The truly cruel thing would have been to let the matter go on festering in Peter so that throughout his entire life both he and the others would think that he was somehow inferior and unworthy of office … the kind thing was the public restoration so that Peter and the others would know that Peter's past was past." [7] Peter's blessing was this — he was restored in front of everyone.

Asking the question, "Do you love me?" reveals our vulnerability. Think about it. How often do we ask "Do you love me?" And to whom? Doesn't it cause our hearts to feel unprotected, to be wide open? Don't we secretly fear what the answer might be?

Our vulnerable Savior asks this question to us. This is our final question to answer.

Pivotal Question #11

Do you love me?

John 21:15-17

Jesus is not through asking questions. On the Damascus road after a blinding light brought Saul to his knees, the first words he heard were a question from Jesus, *Saul, Saul, why are you persecuting me?* [8] It was the question that led Paul to belief. Although blinded, Paul said *he saw Jesus*, the Risen Savior. Paul, blind and stumbling, has nothing for three days but his own internal processing of the vision of the Lord Jesus Christ and His searing question. When Ananias came and laid his hands on Paul, his spiritual blindness had been overcome. He was changed forevermore.

No More Questions

And then there were none. At the end of Scripture Jesus ceases to ask even one question. There are *no questions* in Revelation. *Why?*

Jesus' questions are to reveal myself to me, to reveal Him to me, to bring me face to face with a situation. They are needed to pry away the masks we all wear. They are to bring us to honesty and vulnerability, praying prayers we never have prayed before, having courage to ask for things and admit things we never have before.

Oh yes, there are plenty of questions in Revelation, but it is not Jesus doing the asking. So why in Revelation are there no questions from Jesus?

I don't know.

In Revelation Jesus says seven times, *Whoever has ears, let them hear what the Spirit says to the churches.*[9] Revelation is the final revealing of the Lord Jesus Christ in Holy Scripture and all we need to know is then complete on this side of eternity. We have what we need to know Him. Could it be that it is the time to listen and hear the words of the King?

Revelation ends with a statement from Jesus, *Yes, I am coming soon.*[10] Could it be that Jesus' next questions will be in person?

Jesus asks His questions to reveal to ourselves the very answers we seek. Could it be that **the time is now to answer** His questions hanging unanswered in eternity? Will there come a time, as with the Sanhedrin, when the door closes? All the more reason to answer His questions *now* while there is time, deeply delving into His questions to draw even closer to Him.

Could there come a time when He asks no more questions? I do not believe so. I believe that through eternity the Lord Jesus will continue asking questions in order to reveal Himself more and more fully. Asking questions is built into the fiber of His character. We will never fully know Him. He is eternal, unfathomable, unsearchable, and our delight will be in continuing to know Him for all the ages.

Yet, what about our questions of Him? One final thought comes from John 16:29-30.

> *Then Jesus' disciples said, "Now you are speaking clearly and without figures of speech. Now we can see that you know all things and that you do not even need to have anyone ask you questions. This makes us believe that you came from God."*
>
> *"You believe at last!" Jesus answered.*

There is a connection between questions and belief. Something clicked with the disciples and they believed. Will the same be true of our questions? When we see Him face to face, and see ourselves more clearly, will our questions fall by the wayside? As we know the Lord Jesus Christ more and more, will our questions be silenced? I believe so. Isn't that the case with us right now after answering even a few of His questions? Our questions are silenced when we know and believe Who He Is!

Think on this

The more satisfied in Him,
the more silent our questions become.

He is the Great Answer.

Unless we get hurt right out of every deception about ourselves, the word of God is not having its way with us. The question of the Lord intensifies feeling, until the hurt by Jesus is the most exquisite hurt conceivable. The word of the Lord pierces even to the dividing asunder of soul and spirit, there is no deception left. There never can be any mistake about the hurt of the Lord's word when it comes to His child; but the point of the hurt is the great point of revelation.
-OSWALD CHAMBERS[11]-

Pivotal Question #11

Do you love me?
Matthew 27:46, Mark 15:34

Read *John 21.*

This is the question. The one we knew we would get to. And, I believe, the one all other questions have led us to. *Do we love Him?* Three times He asks Peter. After the third time the apostle John tells us that Peter was hurt. Jesus asked until it hurt. Let's allow Him to ask us until it hurts. Maybe that will be one time, maybe it will be many more. What matters is that in the hurt we become honest and broken, and we surrender.

The sacrifice you desire is a broken spirit. You will not reject a broken and repentant heart, O God. Psalm 51:17 NLT

Before answering, prayerfully read through all your other questions and answers. By now you have answered ten questions. Was there one particular question that was a turning point for you? Were there any questions too hard to answer? Are there questions you are still answering?

Look closely at your answers. Do you see some same phrases, or a theme running through your answers? Did you figure something out along the way? How have the questions changed your relationship with Jesus? Have you found any answers to *your* questions?

If Jesus asked you this question today,
how would you respond to Him?

End Notes

CHAPTER 1

[1] Job 1:8 and Job 42:4-6, *New International Version*

[2] Jeremiah 17:9, *New International Version*

[3] I Samuel 16:7, *New International Version*

[4] C. H. Spurgeon, *God's First Words to the First Sinner*, http://spurgeongems.org/vols7-9/chs412.pdf

[5] John 1:22-23, *New International Version*

[6] John 1:35, *New International Version*

[7] John Dear, *The Questions of Jesus, Challenging Ourselves to Discover Life's Great Answers* (Image Books: Doubleday, 2004), 2. Used by permission.

[8] Suzanne Matthews, March 2014. The very first words I wrote in my own journal while teaching this study for the first time and attempting to answer the eleven questions myself.

CHAPTER 2

[1] Job 9:32-33, *New International Version*

[2] Matthew 4:12, *Holman Christian Standard Bible*

[3] Luke 4:14, *Holman Christian Standard Bible*

[4] Spiros Zodhiates, Th.D., *The Complete Word Study New Testament* (AMG International, Inc.), 1991, pgs. 316, 21.

[5] Exodus 3:14, *New International Version*

[6] John 18:4-6, *New International Version*

[7] John 4:28-29, *Holman Christian Standard Bible*

[8] Joshua 5-6

[9] Matthew 1:5

[10] John 5:1-18, *Holman Christian Standard Bible*

[11] James Montgomery Boice, *The Gospel of John Volume I* (Baker Books, a division of Baker Publishing Group), 2000, pgs. 278-279. Used by permission.

[12] Suzanne Matthews, August 17, 2014. My husband suffered a cardiac arrest on July 25, 2014. Five days later, he regained consciousness and began a long survival journey. Shortly after he came home from the hospital, I taught this study for the second time. Four months prior, I had taught the initial class and answered every question — this excerpt is from my journal when I answered this question *a second time*, four months later. I was at the weakest point of my life, and all I could recall from the class was *believe, believe, believe*. For those very special days I was being carried by God and fear was absent.

CHAPTER 3

[1] Romans 10:17, *New International Version*

[2] Luke 8:25, *Holman Christian Standard Bible*

[3] Mark 5:6-10, *Holman Christian Standard Bible*

[4] Exodus 3:14-15, *The Message*

[5] Mark 5:21-43, *Holman Christian Standard Bible*

[6] Matthew 9:27-31, *Holman Christian Standard Bible*

[7] Isaiah 1:18, New International Version. I am not ashamed to admit Isaiah is my favorite book in the Bible, and on that day a verse from Isaiah 1 came barreling into my memory. I guess I have read that verse so many times that, even in my distress, I did not want to bargain with God (for I have nothing to bargain with); I wanted to *reason* with God.

[8] Luke 7:1-10, *Holman Christian Standard Bible*

[9] Spiros Zodhiates, Th.D., *The Complete Word Study New Testament* (AMG International, Inc.), 1991, pgs. 135, 217, 36.

[10] Mark 6:1-6, *Holman Christian Standard Bible*

[11] John 6:29, *New International Version*

[12] John 6:35-39, *Holman Christian Standard Bible*

[13] Matthew 14:24-33, *Holman Christian Standard Bible*

[14] Matthew 16:13-20, *Holman Christian Standard Bible*

[15] John Dear, *The Questions of Jesus, Challenging Ourselves to Discover Life's Great Answers* (Image Books: Doubleday, 2004), 13-14. Used by permission.

CHAPTER 4

[1] Mark 9:24, *Holman Christian Standard Bible*

[2] Matthew 16:13-21, *Holman Christian Standard Bible*

[3] *English Standard Version Study Bible* (Crossway, Wheaton, Illinois), 2008, pgs. 1856-1857, 1911, 1973.

[4] Luke 9:28-31, *New International Version*

[5] Matthew 17:5-7; Mark 9:7-8; Luke 9:34-36, *Holman Christian Standard Bible*

[6] 2 Peter 1:16-21, *New Living Translation*

[7] Charles Haddon Spurgeon, www.goodreads.com

[8] Mark 9:17-24, *New International Version*

[9] Spiros Zodhiates, Th.D., *The Complete Word Study New Testament* (AMG International, Inc.), 1991, pgs. 150, 14, 58.

[10] John 7:2-10, *New International Version*

[11] John 7:16-19, 28-33, *New International Version*

[12] John 7:37-39, *New International Version*

[13] Gary M. Burge, *Jesus and the Jewish Festivals* (Zondervan, Grand Rapids, Michigan), 2012, pg. 77. Used by permission.

[14] John 8:12, *New International Version*

[15] John 6:29, *New International Version*

[16] Suzanne Matthews, August 28, 2014.

CHAPTER 5

[1] Frank Viola, *God's Favorite Place on Earth*, http://godsfavoriteplace.com. Used by permission.

[2] John 10:22-31, *New International Version*

[3] John 10:40, 42, *New International Version*

[4] James Montgomery Boice, *The Gospel of John Volume III (Baker Books)*, 2000, pg. 802. Used by permission.

[5] John 11:5, *Holman Christian Standard Bible*

[6] John 11:11-15, *New International Version*

[7] James Montgomery Boice, *The Gospel of John Volume III (Baker Books)*, 2000, pg. 828. Used by permission.

[8] John 11:25-26, *Holman Christian Standard Bible*

[9] *English Standard Version Study Bible* (Crossway, Wheaton, Illinois), 2008, pg. 2046.

[10] James Montgomery Boice, *The Gospel of John Volume III* (Baker Books), 2000, pg. 870. Used by permission.

[11] John 11:43, *Holman Christian Standard Bible*

[12] Oswald Chambers, *My Utmost for His Highest* (Barbour and Company, by special arrangement with and permission of Discover House Publishers), 1935, February 7.

[13] I Kings 3:5, *New International Version*. It is worth reading the exchange between God and Solomon, I Kings 3:5-15, for further proof that God is most interested in our heart's desires, and that our answers reveal much.

CHAPTER 6

[1] Francis Bottome, "Search Me, O God" (1823), selected verses.

[2] Mark 14:3-9, *Holman Christian Standard Bible*

[3] Gary M. Burge, *Jesus and the Jewish Festivals* (Zondervan, Grand Rapids, Michigan), 2012, pgs. 107-108. Used by permission.

[4] Luke 22:15-16, *Holman Christian Standard Bible*

[5] Taken from *The Feasts of the Lord* by Kevin Howard and Marvin Rosenthal, 2012, pg. 55. Used by permission from Thomas Nelson, www.thomasnelson.com.

[6] John 13:12, *Holman Christian Standard Bible*

[7] John 13:1, *Holman Christian Standard Bible*

[8] Taken from *The Feasts of the Lord* by Kevin Howard and Marvin Rosenthal, 2012, pg. 57. Used by permission from Thomas Nelson, www.thomasnelson.com.

[9] John 13:26-27, *Holman Christian Standard Bible*

[10] John 13:30, *Holman Christian Standard Bible*

[11] John 13:34, *Holman Christian Standard Bible*

[12] Luke 22:35, *Holman Christian Standard Bible*

[13] Taken from *The Feasts of the Lord* by Kevin Howard and Marvin Rosenthal, 2012, pg. 59. Used by permission from Thomas Nelson, www.thomasnelson.com.

[14] Luke 22:19-20, *Holman Christian Standard Bible*

[15] John 14:1-12, *Holman Christian Standard Bible*

[16] John 14-17.

[17] Gary M. Burge, *Jesus and the Jewish Festivals* (Zondervan, Grand Rapids, Michigan), 2012, pg. 113. Used by permission.

[18] Luke 22:18, *Holman Christian Standard Bible*

[19] Gary M. Burge, *Jesus and the Jewish Festivals* (Zondervan, Grand Rapids, Michigan), 2012, pg. 118. Used by permission.

[20] Suzanne Matthews, April, 2014. I wrote that I was coming to a place where I might ask for more faith. I do not recall ever asking. Whether or not this prayer was ever formed on my lips, in July of 2014, my heart found an answer. My faith grew leaps and bounds through my husband's trauma and miraculous survival of sudden cardiac arrest.

CHAPTER 7

[1] II Corinthians 5:21, *New International Version*

[2] John 16:12, *Holman Christian Standard Bible*

[3] Matthew 26:40, Luke 22:46, *Holman Christian Standard Bible*

[4] Luke 22:45, *Holman Christian Standard Bible*

[5] Luke 22:41-42, *Holman Christian Standard Bible*

[6] Luke 22:44, *Holman Christian Standard Bible*

[7] John 18:4-6, *New International Version*

[8] James Montgomery Boice, *The Gospel of John Volume V* (Baker Books), 2000, pg. 1379. Used by permission.

[9] Luke 22:48, *Holman Christian Standard Bible*

[10] Matthew 26:55, *Holman Christian Standard Bible*

[11] John 18:23, *Holman Christian Standard Bible*

[12] Matthew 26:57-63, Mark 14:53-61, *Holman Christian Standard Bible*

[13] Matthew 26:58-72, *Holman Christian Standard Bible*

[14] Luke 22:60-62, *Holman Christian Standard Bible*

[15] Spiros Zodhiates, Th.D., *The Complete Word Study New Testament* (AMG International, Inc.), 1991, pgs. 292, 28.

[16] William Barclay, *The Gospel of John*, vol. 2 (Philadelphia:Westminster Press, 1956), 269.

[17] Luke 22:67-70, *Holman Christian Standard Bible*

[18] John 18:33-38, *Holman Christian Standard Bible*

[19] John 19:1-11, *Holman Christian Standard Bible*

[20] *English Standard Version Study Bible* (Crossway, Wheaton, Illinois), 2008, pg. 2010.

[21] Luke 23:34, 39-43; John 19:25-27, *Holman Christian Standard Bible*

[22] Matthew 27:46, Mark 15:34, *Holman Christian Standard Bible*

[23] James Montgomery Boice, *The Gospel of John Volume V* (Baker Books), 2000, pg. 1511. Used by permission.

[24] Matthew 28:20, *New International Version*

CHAPTER 8

[1] James Montgomery Boice, *The Gospel of John Volume V* (Baker Books, a division of Baker Publishing Group), 2000, pgs. 1627-8. Used by permission.

[2] John 20:15, Luke 24:38, *Holman Christian Standard Bible*

[3] John 21:5, *Holman Christian Standard Bible*

[4] John 21:15, *Holman Christian Standard Bible*

[5] John 21:15-17, *Holman Christian Standard Bible*

[6] Spiros Zodhiates, Th.D., *The Complete Word Study New Testament* (AMG International, Inc.), 1991, pgs. 388, 45.

[7] James Montgomery Boice, *The Gospel of John Volume V* (Baker Books), 2000, pg. 1638. Used by permission.

[8] Acts 9:4, New International Version

[9] Revelation 2-3

[10] Revelation 22:20, New International Version

[11] Oswald Chambers, *My Utmost for His Highest* (Barbour and Company, by special arrangement with and permission of Discover House Publishers), 1935, March 1.

Acknowledgements

Thank you, *Jenny Kopp Curl* — for getting my edits started, but most of all, for mentioning to me that teaching the study one last time to a small focus group might be just what was needed for final edits. God spoke through you that day.

My heart to you, *Lane Tutt* — for inviting and re-inviting me to teach at Church of the Nativity, and to the wonderful ladies in the class, many in the beloved *Libba Walker Class.* I'll never forget that first class night, just weeks after Ben's cardiac arrest — I was so raw and weak. You all loved me back to normal.

To the summer focus group — *Karen Brennan, Linda Hargrove, Elizabeth Jones, Laura Martin, Nicole Reeves, Brenda Stout, Katie Taylor, Carolyn Tweedy, and Shelley Whitney* — thank you for your valuable input and suggestions, primarily the new name. I will never forget our evenings at the cabin, and nothing is seared into my memory more than that Sunday afternoon sitting around Carolyn's dining table, hearing testimonies and talking about Passover.

To *Andrea Wilhelm* — praise and gratitude for all the times you read my mind and your design completed my thoughts. You are a joy!

To *my dearest family and friends, you know who you are* — you are the ones who walked the walk with me. You sent emails and cards spurring me on, called to check on me, met me in Monteagle, took me to Nantucket, celebrated book milestones and deadlines at the beach and in the mountains. Most of all, you asked questions. You cared.

And to *Ben* — before 2014, I would have thanked you for all the ways you have supported my writing and my teaching over the years. What sticks in my mind are all those BSF Tuesday nights when you fed and bathed kids, supervised homework, carted to basketball and soccer games, and were a fantastic stand-in for mom, actually lots of times better than mom. But since 2014, your story of survival is my story of faith. Your story is mine; this one of mine is yours.

I loved you dearly. Not content to just pass on the Message,
I wanted to give you my heart. And I did.
I Thessalonians 2:8 *The Message,* with my edits

CPSIA information can be obtained
at www.ICGtesting.com
Printed in the USA
FSOW04n1236090217
30581FS